Learning C.

City and Islington College
Marlborough Building
383 Holloway Road N7 0RN
tel. 020 7700 9283

CITY AND ISLINGTON
COLLEGE

- *This book is due for return on or before the date last stamped below.*
- *You may renew by telephone. Please quote the Barcode No.*
- *May not be renewed if required by another reader.*

Fine: 5p per day

xford
trans-
shing

..ord in the early
of v: isection and
tions into the
human medicines
justified, extensive
cal/scientific value
The present book

is   K *Anti-Vivisection*
ared on television and radio
e for a total, immediate and
ction.

VIVISECTION UNVEILED

An Exposé of the Medical Futility
of Animal Experimentation

Dr. Tony Page

Foreword by Professor Pietro Croce

JON CARPENTER

First published 1997 by Jon Carpenter Publishing,
The Spendlove Centre, Charlbury OX7 3PQ (01608 811969)

The right of Tony Page to be identified as author of this work has been
asserted in accordance with the Copyright, Designs and Patents Act 1988

© Tony Page 1997

ISBN 1 897766 31 9

Printed and bound in England by J W Arrowsmith Ltd., Bristol

Dedicated to the memory of

Dr. Walter R. Hadwen
(1854-1932)

Britain's first great scientific anti-vivisectionist

An enduring beacon of light, goodness and service
in a world misguidedly darkened by worship of self

And hark! how blithe the throstle sings!
He, too, is no mean preacher:
Come forth into the light of things,
Let Nature be your Teacher.

She has a world of ready wealth,
Our minds and hearts to bless –
Spontaneous wisdom breathed by health,
Truth breathed by cheerfulness.

One impulse from a vernal wood
May teach you more of man,
Of moral evil and of good,
Than all the sages can.

Sweet is the lore which Nature brings;
Our meddling intellect
Mis-shapes the beauteous forms of things:–
We murder to dissect.

William Wordsworth, *The Tables Turned*, 1798

Contents

Acknowledgements

First, I should like to thank the great, unsurpassed anti-vivisectionist writer and vivisection chronicler, Hans Ruesch, for initiating a world-wide movement of scientific anti-vivisectionism which is now taking firm root. His seminal work on vivisection — *Slaughter of the Innocent* — still, in my view, stands supreme, like some towering Everest, against which all other peaks in this area must be measured.

Next I wish to give my very warmest and deepest thanks to Professor Pietro Croce, ex-vivisector and the world's leading authority on scientific anti-vivisection. Professor Croce has been uniquely selfless and generous in supporting the present book and urging its dissemination far and wide. This brave and scholarly man, who renounced vivisection on account of its medical uselessness and dangers, is possessed of great humility and integrity and is a rare treasure in our world. Thank you, Pietro, for all your kind assistance and guidance.

Dr. Vernon Coleman has my warm thanks and gratitude for the backing he has given to this book. His writing and public lectures have been a source of vitalising encouragement and inspiration to me.

I should like to extend my thanks also to Mr. Henry Turtle, who first introduced me to the inspirational works and life of the late, great Dr. Walter R. Hadwen. Mr Turtle has done more than any person in Britain to keep the memory of the *real* Dr. Hadwen alive.

Gratitude, too, to Dr. Peter Simmons for his fine 'Reflections' on vivisection (written for this book) and for his help in providing me with some very useful facts.

Dr. André Menache, President of the international organisation, 'Doctors and Lawyers for Responsible Medicine', is warmly thanked for his kind help and extremely valuable information on xenotransplantation. Dr. Michael Antoniou is thanked in this connection likewise.

Professor Vernon Reynolds of Oxford University has my gratitude for his generous assistance regarding chimpanzee data, plus his much valued backing of the central thesis advanced by *Vivisection Unveiled*.

Ms. Rosalind Leitch of the Wagner Society, London, receives my thanks for supplying me with relevant materials relating to Wagner's anti-vivisectionism.

A special expression of gratitude goes to the wonderful Carol Norton for her painstaking, patient and superbly professional preparation of the MS of *Vivisection Unveiled* for publication.

My deepest gratitude goes to the unwaveringly loyal Mrs. Andrea Lewis, a splendid anti-vivisectionist, who has been uniquely encouraging of all my efforts to speak out *scientifically* against vivisection and unsurpassedly supportive during the composition of *Vivisection Unveiled*. Thank you, Andrea, very much indeed.

Thanks also to Mrs. Carole Zdesar for her constant help and commitment to the anti-vivisection cause.

Mrs. Cynthia O'Neill kindly donated a copy of Brandon Reines' excellent book on heart research (referred to in the present work), and also gave much support. Thank you.

Naturopath, Patrick Rattigan, ND, freely supplied lots of practical advice for the maintenance of my health during my years of intensive research on this book, and has my gratitude.

Mr. Julian Davidson, one of the nation's most indefatigable and ubiquitous campaigners against animal abuse, introduced me to the enormously important work of Professor Pietro Croce, and has my thanks.

Mrs. Jill Russell, DCR, a superb anti-vivisectionist researcher and campaigner, has my heartfelt gratitude for her extraordinary generosity, humility and dedication to the anti-vivisection cause. Her help with the preparation of this book has been invaluable.

Mr. Tyrone Kelly provided financial assistance and displayed enormous enthusiasm over *Vivisection Unveiled*, for which I offer him my cordial thanks.

I would like also to thank Jon Carpenter for finding some merit in this book and agreeing to publish it. Many thanks indeed.

Of course my own family have fully backed my endeavours to expose vivisection for the unscientific and medically worthless practice that it in truth constitutes. My thanks extend to them, as always.

Lastly, never-ending gratitude to the man (long since gone from us) who for me is the paragon of all a scientific anti-vivisectionist should be: the benevolent, selfless and brave pioneer, Dr. Walter R. Hadwen. It is his flame (re-kindled, fanned and fed by Hans Ruesch) that is still burning brightly today. Wherever you are, Dr. Hadwen: THANK YOU WITH ALL MY HEART.

Foreword

From this book a hail of stones comes crashing down upon vivisection, some heavy like boulders, others precise and exact like bullets shot by a precision carbine. These stones are facts, facts and again facts, which implacably hit their target.

The book starts by explaining the meaning of the term 'vivisection', though nowadays most people know the appalling reality implied by it. But many, all too many, still believe that vivisection protects humanity from diseases. It does not.

The examples quoted in the first chapter erase this platitude, stressing that stupidity and bad faith are the real motive springs propelling medical research into vivisection, *an aberrant path*. The examples are appalling and irrefutably documented:

... a 4 mm. diameter Teflon-coated probe was stuck up the vagina of unanaesthetized female cats ... (year 1993).

Question: could anybody fail to recognise the sadistic motivation of that particular torture?

... Rats were forced to become drunk by being given sufficient amounts of alcohol ...

Could anybody deny the predictability of that 'experiment'?

... The stomach of cats was exposed to digestive enzymes ... to see bleeding points and erosions. No mention is made of any anaesthetic being given.

... Starvational exhaustion: young guinea-pigs were deprived of adequate amounts of vitamin C ...

Question: did they expect anything but scurvy?

... Eight monkeys were asphyxiated at birth for 7-10 minutes to see what effect this would have upon them ...

Did they expect the monkeys to ask for a diver's oxygen mask?

To see 'what will happen' is the rule rather than the exception among researchers. But that curiosity is at the expense of the community. Taxpayers, remember this next time you pay your taxes!

A crucial question: Are animals suitable experimental models of human beings? The answer is an emphatic *No!* and this book explains why.

Dr. Page is never short of overwhelming evidence to substantiate his statements. The implicit significance of Chapter Two is that *no animal species is a suitable experimental model for humans;* each animal species can be a suitable model only of itself (cats are the only suitable model of the species 'cat'; dogs of the species 'dog', rabbits of the species 'rabbit' ...) — let alone the individual differences, which are clearly detectable in all animal species, just as in humans. This basic concept is highlighted in the third and fifth chapters, again with a harvest of examples.

Upon reading *Vivisection Unveiled*, I almost feel sorry for the unfortunate vivisectionists. But one could rightly object that I should rather feel sorry for those who are paying for the failures of a method which will never solve problems endangering human life, such as cancer, or making the quality of life unbearable, such as arthritis, numerous neurological disorders and other chronic ailments.

Cancer

Could anybody be satisfied with the 'progress' made by research based on animal experimentation in curing, or even in having acquired a better understanding of, cancer? Could anybody be satisfied with a *methodological error?*

The answer is given at the beginning of the sixth chapter: 'For well over 100 years, the vivisectors have been torturing animals to death with artificially induced cancers, in a quest to halt this scourge amongst humankind. With what results? Cancer is now occurring at the rate of 1 in 3 persons in Britain and America'. However, we must admit that the various therapies have apparently achieved a seeming extension of patient survival — *apparently.* I stress that word. In fact, I can explain these seemingly favourable results. The real reason lies paradoxically in the precocity of the diagnosis, that very fact which is commonly considered the main pillar of an efficacious cure: an early diagnosis makes only for *apparently* prolonged survival, by simply commencing the counting of years of survival from an earlier point.

This little digression is aimed at endorsing the sixth chapter of *Vivisection Unveiled*, where it is stressed: 'There has been no significant increase in survival rates since records began ...', etc.

Dr. Page, you are a Doctor of Philosophy. May I ask you, without seeming indiscreet, from where have you acquired your astonishing medical learning?

Professor Pietro Croce
Professor of Pathology, Vicenza, Italy. 15 November 1996

Reflections on Vivisection
by a GP

It is strange that concern for animals is often taken as a sign of sentimentality and weakness. Maybe this is because loving animals is innate in most children, and therefore seen as something to 'grow out of', something childish and immature. As we 'mature' we are taught to view animals in a more 'realistic' way. The biblical description of Man as having 'dominion' over the beasts and fishes and fowls is taken as meaning not stewardship but domination. Animals are provided for us to use as we find convenient, for food, sport, clothing, and tools in our laboratories.

So it was that I, a child who wrote passionate verses against cruelty to animals, matured into a medical student conducting physiology experiments on living animals as part of my routine training to become a caring doctor. A frog is firmly grasped and as a prelude to the experiment is 'pithed'. A long needle is pushed into the fully conscious frog's brain and wiggled about, mashing the brain to a pulp. While this is done, the animal's legs struggle helplessly, and its eyes move in and out of their sockets. Later, a technician clubs a rabbit to death in front of the class of teenagers, and not one protests. All this to perform experiments which have been repeated by students for decades, including no doubt by my father and by my grandfather. But of course the experiments were very useful, they taught me to detach myself from my feelings while inflicting pain. After all, a doctor must not become too emotionally involved with his/her patients!

When I first heard about vivisection as a child I could not believe that such things could happen. I felt that they were some kind of invented myth. Later, when I discovered that they did indeed happen (and worse things than I could imagine), I was conned by the establishment belief that without them medical progress would be slow or non-existent. But when I researched the subject, reading Hans Ruesch, Robert Sharpe and others, as well as the books putting the case for animal experiments, I realised that there didn't have to be a conflict between heart and head. There have been innumerable debates on the rights and wrongs of animal experiments, usually based on the supposition that they are essential, and so concentrating on the moral dilemmas. They make marvellous material for radio or television, but are ultimately pointless except as an intellectual exercise, as it boils down to 'this mouse or your child', and human nature generally makes the predictable choice!

But what if they are not essential? What if they are actually harmful to people as well as to animals, because they give the wrong answers due to species differences? In this book, Dr. Page gives yet more damning evidence that differences between species make it impossible to extrapolate results from one species to another. He describes in fascinating detail how there are so many differences even between different species of monkey, that results from one type of monkey cannot even be applied to another type of monkey. Hence claims that veterinary medicine benefits from animal experiments are given the lie.

So here are a few more shovelfuls of facts to heap on the grave of that old vampire Vivisection, that feeds on the blood of living creatures, and that separates us from the unity with all living things that is vital for our spiritual well-being and true health. Dr. Page writes with emotion and passion, because he writes from deep conviction. He gave up a successful academic career to devote himself to the subject. But beneath the emotion is hard-headed fact and detailed, well-referenced research. He shows us the scientific worthlessness of animal experiments, and his book is a valuable addition to the growing mountain of scientific anti-vivisectionist literature. He goes further, and enlists the support of the vivisectors themselves. With extensive quotes he shows how even they realise the uselessness of their own research. For once, I can agree with these pseudo-scientists, and as a practising doctor, disregard totally their dangerously misleading 'results'. I hope that this book will help others to reach the same conclusion.

Dr Peter Simmons, M.B., B.S.
Former Vice-President, Doctors in Britain Against Animal Experiments
Quondam Member of the Scientific Advisory Committee of the RSPCA

Introduction

Vivisection (animal experimentation) has countless deaths upon its conscience — both animal and human. But, then, vivisection has no conscience in truth — or at best, a tragically misguided one.

Increasing numbers of concerned citizens throughout the world are now objecting to vivisection, and amongst their ranks are to be found numerous doctors, scientists, artists and scholars who oppose animal 'research' not simply on moral grounds but on strong *scientific* and *medical* ones too. It is the specific purpose of the present work to present that scientific evidence, drawn largely from the pens of the experimenters themselves, in sufficient quantities as to damn the practice of vivisection beyond reasonable doubt. We will hear the voices of doctors, ex-vivisectors and vivisection-supporting researchers (who may at some point in the past have been involved in animal tests themselves) effectively condemning this unscientific cult of blood sacrifices. We shall also be able to weigh the words of practising vivisectors who, when pushed into a corner or when they think the general public is not likely to read or hear what they say in their specialist journals or at their occasional symposia, confess the enormous problems they are having trying to make work an essentially unworkable system. Their testimony is particularly revealing.

No book on this subject can fairly omit mention of two pioneering giants in the field of scientific anti-vivisectionism: the first is the late, great and selfless physician, Dr. Walter R. Hadwen, who was the first to state repeatedly and insistently that the battle against vivisection will only be won if it is fought *scientifically* and who devoted the latter half of his life to tireless campaigning against the medical *inutility* of animal experimentation. The second giant is the great anti-vivisection writer and trenchant critic of vivisectionist medicine, Hans Ruesch, who took over from where the brilliant Dr. Hadwen left off and advanced the movement further by focusing on the tremendous *dangers* of vivisection for humankind and by highlighting those 'anti-vivisection' organisations that, either through infiltrational treachery or unpardonable intellectual laziness, refused to argue the anti-vivisection case scientifically. The RSPCA — despite the commendable efforts of doctors such as Dr. Peter

Simmons — is equally culpable, having throughout its existence effectively *supported* vivisection in its broad, general sweep.

The present small book can never approximate or even approach the merits enshrined in the seminal writings of the heroic figures, Dr. Hadwen and Hans Ruesch; but it may perhaps serve as a useful little supplement to what those illustrious progenitors of the genuine anti-vivisection movement have already taught us.

Some of what follows will be very technical, but I ask the reader to 'press on regardless', as it does get easier towards the end! If the reader feels s/he is getting bogged down in scientific minutiae, s/he is advised to hold fast to the golden thread that runs through virtually every page and paragraph of the book: the fact that in many unforeseen and unforeseeable ways animals have proven themselves to be biologically distinct from human beings — in a word, they are different from us (as well as from one another across the species boundaries). As long as that key point of unpredictable difference is grasped, the meaning and movement of all my arguments will be grasped too.

Now it is time to turn to the arguments and jigsaw-pieces of evidence themselves. I trust you will approach the following pages with an open mind — with what the great dramatist, Friedrich Schiller (in his 'magnum opus', *Wallenstein*), calls a 'willing ear and eye'. Thank you.

CHAPTER ONE

The Experiments

Vivisection is the experimentation upon *living* beings, animal or human, for the alleged benefit of beings other than that specific individual. Generally the word is used to refer to *animal* experiments, whether or not cutting is involved, and that is how we shall mainly use it here.

What types of experiment have been performed? Innumerable. Almost every form of stupidity, harm, suffering and torture that can be inflicted upon a living creature has, at some time, in some place, been inflicted upon animals in the vivisection laboratories. Here are a few examples, chosen at random:

FEAR! The vivisectors wanted to instil sustained fear into rats to see how they would behave, so they soaked a cloth with cats' odour (cats are natural predators of rats and mice) and placed it in a rat cage for up to an hour. To the astonishment of the 'scientists' the rats, confronted with a perceived threat to their lives, cowered away under the food and water container in terror, whereas those rats not exposed to this phobic-stimulant did not display such fear. This was done in 1994 at Guy's Hospital in London.[1]

RAPE! The Royal Veterinary College in London (yes, they are into vivisection too!) carried out the following experiment on cats: a 4 mm diameter Teflon probe was stuck up the vagina of unanaesthetized female cats until the cats cried out in protest. The cats were 'restrained' so as not to be able to break free and escape. A 1 mm diameter ball-tipped *needle* was also stuck into the hapless creatures to a depth of 40 mm. This was reported in 1993.[2]

DRUNKENNESS! Rats were forced to become drunk by being given sufficient amounts of alcohol and then made to walk along a swaying horizontal bar. The researchers found that alcohol '… impairs animal's performance in a dose-related manner'.[3] Such useful information! And this in 1994.

STOMACH LACERATION! The vivisectors wanted to see if certain human pepsins (digestive enzymes in the stomach) caused bleeding in the cat's stomach, so they stuck these enzymes onto the exposed cat stomach and every 15 minutes counted up all the bleeding-points and erosions that they had caused. No mention is made in the Abstract of any anaesthetic being given.[4]

STARVATIONAL EXHAUSTION! Young guinea-pigs were deprived of adequate amounts of Vitamin C for healthy bodily functioning and their diets were severely restricted for *eight weeks* to see, amongst other things, how this would affect the animals' growth. The vivisectors were also keen to chart the stages of inanition (*exhaustion*, brought about by *starvation*) associated with such experiments.[5]

INFECTION OF CATS THROUGH SHEER 'INADVERTENCY'! The Department of Veterinary Medicine (yes, the 'vets' again!) at the University of Bristol presided over the 'inadvertent' infection of 19 experimental cats with the feline calicivirus.[6] Thirteen of those cats had already been infected with feline immunodeficiency virus — the cat equivalent of human AIDS. The animals developed chronic gingivitis (inflammation of the gums) and the researchers concluded that of the cats infected with the AIDS-like virus *and* feline calicivirus, and those cats which only had one of the two viruses, 'the gingivitis was generally more severe in the cats infected with both viruses ...'[6] Extraordinary! We also wonder where these vivisectors' famed (but utterly useless) Home Office 'licence' for this experimentation was when, through sheer 'inadvertency' (another name for which is 'negligence'), they allowed cats to be damaged by a very nasty virus.

Of course animals are routinely infected with all manner of viruses, maladies and diseases in the vivisection laboratories. Experiments to create cancer in animals are legion, and can include injecting cancer into them and the painting of parts of their bodies with carcinogenic (cancer-causing) substances — experiments which one typically sensitive vivisector has referred to as '... play[ing] games with mouse skin and rabbit ears'.[7] Virtually all new medicines and industrial chemicals are also 'tested out' on animals, as are many weapons and agents of war. Yet even the non-military experiments are often startlingly cruel (and always pointless). For example:

Intense electric shocks were given to 36 3-week-old chicks to see what would happen to them.[8]

Eight monkeys were asphyxiated at birth for 7-10 minutes to see what effects this would have upon them.[9]

Vivisectors made incisions (cuts) in the eyes of 45 dogs and 47 rabbits and studied what happened to those damaged eyes over a period of 7 days.[10]

Scottish experimenters pushed fine polythene tubes into rats' brains and then inflated balloons inside the animals' heads.[11]

Rats' tails were immersed in hot water in an experiment on pain ...[12]

We could easily go on, drawing examples from the annals of vivisection. But the point is surely clear: animal experiments are cruel and stupid. Even the Research Defence Society (the vivisectors' PR organisation in Britain) stated recently (in eccentric grammar):

'... there is no doubt that pain and distress occurs [sic!] in laboratory animals' (*RDS News*, October 1996).

After the pain and distress, death is of course the inevitable destination of laboratory animals. Some experimenters have coldly spoken of the vivisectors' slaughter of animals in terms of 'serial killings' (e.g. Dr. David Clayson and Dr. Morris Cranmer in Dr. F. Coulston's book referred to in Chapter Six), and at least one vivisector, as recently as the early 1990s, admitted that killing animals was akin to '... recreational sex because you do it without much feeling ... there's not really a second thought for that animal as an individual' (vivisector quoted by Arnold Arluke in *New Scientist*, 4 April 1992). Such a callous statement requires no further commentary.

Clearly, suffering, distress and death are the ineluctable concomitants of animal experimentation. Yet are these animal tests 'scientific' in their nature and useful to humans in their results?

CHAPTER TWO

Why Animal Experiments Do Not Work and Cannot Work

A nimals are in numerous ways biologically different from humans. They look different from us, they *are* different from us — genetically, anatomically, physiologically, histologically, metabolically, and a lot more besides. Plain common sense, isn't it? Yet the vivisectors have spent the last 150 years attempting to brainwash the public into a vague and crazy notion of mice, rats, dogs, cats, armadillos, rabbits, fish, birds (and others) all being miniature mock-ups of humans and suitable 'models' for human-health research. It is time to do what the great philosopher, Kant, urged and look at the *evidence* and think for ourselves: 'Have the courage to make use of your own intelligence!'[13] Kant recommended.

Different animal and human diseases

Firstly, animals do not suffer from all the same diseases as humankind. Of the *30,000* known human diseases (Bayer drug company advertisement, *The Independent*, 14.11.94), animals would seem to share only around *1.16%* of them, if the apologists for vivisection, such as Britain's 'Research Defence Society', are correct when they boast that approximately 350 illnesses are analogous (shared) between animals and humankind. This is a paltry number when measured against the thousands and thousands of diseases with which humans can be afflicted. Even if the disease is *similar* (which of course does not mean *identical*), there may be important aetiological and symptom-specific differences. This helps account for the fact that approaching *two thirds* of the medicines prescribed for animals are *different* from those prescribed for people.[14] If a laboratory animal does not normally and naturally suffer from a 'human'-type disease, and the vivisectors want to use that animal as a model of that particular disease, they must first try artificially to create a similar disease in their test subject. How is this done? Sometimes by violent physical means (hammer blows to the body of the animal, for example), but more usually by the injection of various chemicals in an attempt to 'mimic' (a favourite vivisectionist word) the malady manifested in humans.[15] If we take the degenerative human illness, multiple sclerosis, for instance, we find the experimenters confronted with an ailment which animals do not naturally contract, so the 'scientists' are forced to create an artificial disease called 'chronic relapsing experimental allergic encephalomyelitis', which according to the Multiple Sclerosis Society of Great Britain and Northern Ireland 'bears *some* resemblance to MS'.[16] (Emphasis added). The word 'resemblance' means 'similarity' *not* 'identity', and this state of affairs is further watered down by the adjective, 'some'. So even the alleged similarity is here revealed as being not so similar to multiple sclerosis after all! Can we imagine a more foolish approach than trying to find a cure for a human disease, the causes of which are *unknown*, by artificially creating an animal ailment which is not only not the human illness but not even very similar to it in the first place?!

Animal reactions to food and chemicals

It gets worse, however, since we must now remember that one of the chief purposes of vivisection is to find 'cures' (or at least treatments) for human diseases. To this end drugs are developed using animals as experimental testing kits and to determine safe and effective dosages for human patients. It is in this area that vivisection displays its most stunning inappropriateness and dangers, since animals (on account of their many physiological deviations from ourselves) *frequently respond unpredictably differently from humans to food, drugs and other chemicals.* Thus no vivisector can *ever reliably predict whether the action of a drug will be the same in a human as in a laboratory animal.* He/she can only *guess.* What kind of 'science' should we term that? Gambling? Russian roulette?!

It may come as a surprise to the reader to learn that there is an all but inexhaustible list of variations between animals and people when it comes to their capacity to 'stomach' a food or chemical. What is safe at one relative dosage for an animal may be deadly for a human. Let us look at a few (out of many) examples of how animals are strikingly different from us in what they can tolerate.

The plant, 'Deadly Nightshade', does not bear that ominous name for nothing: it is highly poisonous to human beings. Yet some strains of rabbit can eat it to their hearts' content with no ill effects.

Hemlock, which the philosopher, Socrates, famously drank to kill himself, can be consumed in large amounts by horses, goats, sheep and mice.

The 'Deathcap Toadstool' ('Amanita phalloides') is one of the most poisonous fungi known; yet rabbits can eat it with impunity.

Botulinum poison will easily terminate the life of anyone who partakes of it, but cats can swallow it and come back for more! The mouse, however, is extraordinarily sensitive to botulinum: remarkably, just 1 mg (about the size of a tiny vitamin pill) is said to be enough to kill 20 million mice (this is reported in *The Dose Makes the Poison*, Vincente Books, 1984, by the vivisector, Dr. M. Ottoboni). But the cat which is immune to botulinum will drop down dead if generously fed with lemon juice, as will some rabbits.[17]

Antimony is a metal which if ingested by us will kill us but it will not kill pigs; on the contrary, it will fatten them up!

Methyl alcohol causes blindness in people, but not in any non-primate animal that has been studied.

Strychnine is highly dangerous for humans, yet can be tolerated and survived (in amounts proportional to body-weight much greater than that able to be survived by humans) by chickens, guinea-pigs, rabbits and long-tailed monkeys.

Vitamin C is essential in our diets if we are not to die of scurvy, but it is not needed in the diets of dogs, cats, rats, mice and hamsters, since they can synthesize Vitamin C inside their own bodies.

Prussic acid, the very fumes of which will kill us, can be ingested by toads, sheep and hedgehogs.

Most extraordinary of all is the case of cats and dogs and the poisonous alkaloid, scopolamine: just 5 milligrams of scopolamine will spell death to a human, but cats and dogs can take up to 100 mg and survive. If we calculate the lethal doses according to the relative body weights (which is the usual way of determining dosages) of cats, dogs and people, we find that the cat and dog can in effect (relative to their size) tolerate the equivalent of 1,800 mg of scopolamine, which is a dose approximately 360 times greater than that which will kill a human!

Other substances and chemicals can also vary enormously in their respective effects upon animals and humans:

Amyl nitrite raises the internal pressure in dogs' eyes, but reduces it in human eyes.

Insulin causes birth defects in chickens, rabbits and mice, but human diabetics have been using insulin for decades without its having this effect upon their babies.

Digitalis was once discouraged from use in human patients because it raised the blood pressure of dogs: in fact, in humans it has the reverse effect — it lowers the blood pressure and has been used effectively in many cases of heart disease.

Cicloserine is useless against experimental tuberculosis ('TB') in guinea-pigs and mice, but has proven helpful in the treatment of TB in humans.

Chloramphenicol can seriously damage the blood-producing bone marrow in human patients (causing the fatal condition aplastic anaemia), but this does not happen in laboratory animals.

The industrial chemical, TOCP, damages nerve fibres in humans and chickens, but not in dogs or rats (see Dr. Ottoboni, p.49).

The chemical, nitrobenzene, can seriously damage the blood's oxygen transport function in people, cats and dogs — but not in monkeys (our close relatives), rats and rabbits (favourite laboratory animals) (Ottoboni, p.49).

The dioxin chemical, TCDD, is one of the most toxic chemicals for animals created by humans. Yet the lethal doses between different animal species vary considerably: guinea pigs will be despatched by just 0.6 microg/kg, whereas chickens can tolerate up to 50 microg/kg, and dogs and rats can survive anything from 100 to 200 microg/kg. Yet humans appear to be far less susceptible to the harmful effects of TCDD than all of these animals (Ottoboni, pp.147-151).

It is hardly surprising that humans should often be so different from animals in what substances, and how much of them, they can ingest without being fatally harmed, since animals themselves vary enormously from species to species (as we have already glimpsed); even individuals of the same species can vary significantly. To illustrate species variation amongst animals, let us consider the following disparate doses of chemicals sufficient to kill some species of animal but not others:

Dogs can survive an intravenous injection of 300 mg per kilo of their own body weight of the chemical, acetanilide, but cats will be killed by just 13.5 mg/kg. Yet the mouse can survive around 8 times as much acetanilide as the cat.[18]

Rabbits can eat up to 100 mg/kg of digitoxin, but the cat (a comparably sized creature) will drop down dead if it swallows just 0.25 mg/kg — that is a four-hundred-fold difference![19]

Rabbits can consume a minimum dose of 590 mg/kg of ephedrine before giving up the ghost, but it only takes 160 mg/kg to send a rat into an early grave. The behavioural effects induced by the ingestion of ephedrine manifest themselves at even more contrasting levels: behavioural changes will become apparent in rats at 100 mg/kg but dogs will display behavioural modifications when given a mere 0.006 mg/kg.[20] Another enormous variation.

It takes a large intravenous injection of 85 mg/kg of methylergonovine to kill a mouse, but a mere 2.6 mg/kg is sufficient to do the job in rabbits.[21]

A dog can be killed by eating 1.6 mg/kg of potassium cyanide, but a rabbit can tolerate 5 mg/kg, and a mouse can survive a dose of 16 mg/kg.[22]

We have already noted the deadly effects of scopolamine, but let us see how much it takes of this substance to exert a sedative effect upon mice and rats: mice cannot be sedated with anything much less than 450 mg/kg, but rats only require 13 mg/kg.[23]

Strychnine is another deadly poison already alluded to, and we might now examine in a little more detail the tolerance ability of the rabbit as regards this noxious alkaloid of the *Strychnos nux-vomica* tree: rabbits can swallow up to 15 mg/kg of strychnine before it kills them[24], whereas human beings can be killed by 0.5 mg/kg (30 mg in absolute terms, according to Dr. Bernard Knight's *Simpson's Forensic Medicine*, 1991, p.310). We thus see that the rabbit can survive (relative to body weight) something like 30 times the amount of strychnine that humans can. Even those humans who have required as much as 100 mg of strychnine to kill them[25] are still inferior (given their much greater body weight) to the humble rabbit! Yet even rabbits cannot tolerate as much subcutaneously injected strychnine as the mouse, which can take 1.33 mg/kg before convulsions wrack its body, whereas the rabbit will suffer the onset of convulsions at just 0.4 mg/kg of subcutaneously injected strychnine. The dog is even weaker in this regard, as it will be stricken with convulsions after being subcutaneously injected with as little as 0.07 mg/kg of strychnine.[26] With such variations, how can the vivisectors know what amounts of a substance can safely be tolerated by the differently constituted human being? The answer is: they cannot. They can only guess. The man/woman in the street can do that — but he/she is not paid a handsome salary for indulging in dangerous guessing-games (unlike the vivisectors).

The notorious drug, Thalidomide, which caused such tragic birth deformities in human babies, also has a depressive effect upon the central nervous system ('CNS'): mice will suffer 'CNS' depression after an intra-peritoneal injection of 500 mg/kg, yet the dog will be affected by as little as 65 mg/kg.[27] As regards Thalidomide's ability to generate damage in the human being, it has been stated in the *Journal of the American Medical Association* (October 20 1975) that humans have been found to be 60 times more sensitive to Thalidomide than mice, 100 times more sensitive than rats, 200 times more sensitive than dogs, and 700 times more sensitive than hamsters![28] So what do animal tests tell us except one thing: not to place any faith in this foolhardy system of trying to transfer animal data to human beings. Vivisection is not, and can never be, predictive. The equation animal = human has been demonstrated to be dangerously false over and over again.

Finally, we might consider the organic compound, histamine. Rabbits (the heroes of oral strychnine ingestion) will be killed by a subcutaneous injection of only 13.5 mg/kg of this substance, whereas the little mouse will survive up to 2,500 mg/kg![29] And human beings? Who knows? The vivisectors certainly don't ...

CHAPTER THREE

Further Examples of Species Variation

We have begun to gain some startling insights into the wide physiological differences between various animal species, and animals and humans. So central is this fact to an understanding of why vivisection is doomed to producing at best useless, time-wasting (because always inconclusive) results and at worst deadly failure that we need to explore further avenues of difference in this chapter. We shall look at anatomical, physiological and behavioural variations as between different animal species themselves, and animals and humankind.

The great apes

In a book on primate biology, co-edited by the marvellously named vivisectionist, Dr. Swindler (!), we learn of significant differences between those animals that are said to be closest to humans in the tree of evolution: monkeys and apes.

The orang-utan bears a sufficiently strong outward resemblance to the human being for it to have been named the 'wild man' by the Malays (this is the meaning of 'orang-utan' in the Malay language). Yet the two main kinds of orang-utan are different in striking ways from each other.

The Bornean and Sumatran orang-utans, we learn, display very numerous and thoroughgoing differences, according to Dr. Colin P. Groves.[30] Dr. Groves lists among those differences the fact that the face of the Bornean orang is broader than that of the Sumatran orang, and has an 8-shaped face with a projecting jaw, whereas the Sumatran orang has an O-shaped face with a flatter jaw. The braincase of the Bornean orang is longer than that of the Sumatran, and the jaws of the male are broader. The 'beard' which the Bornean male vainly sports upon its chin is sparse, whereas the Sumatran male always boasts a well-developed beard with a long moustache. The Bornean orang tends towards obesity, but its enviable cousin from Sumatra is possessed of a linear and muscular body-type. On the other hand, the Bornean orang-utan has almost no hair on its face, while the Sumatran's face is noticeably hairy. More interestingly, the mating habits are different: whereas the Bornean orang enters into only a short-lived bond with its mate, the more monogamously inclined Sumatran orang will maintain a long-lasting bond with its chosen partner. Even the calls of the two primates are different: the male Bornean ape has a loud, long and drawn-out call, but its Sumatran relative emits a shorter, rhythmically faster cry. Their very mode of walking varies too: the Bornean orang-utan has never been found frequently to walk upright like a human or to strut along, but such bipedal 'strutting' is commonly found in the Sumatran ape — a kind of would-be John Travolta, we might say![31]

It is not only the orang-utan which varies markedly within its own family: gorillas do too. If we compare two types of gorilla, the *Gorilla gorilla gorilla* and the *Gorilla gorilla beringei*, we find that the hair on the scalp of the first-named is short, but on the other it is long and shaggy, as is the hair of the brows, whereas *Gorilla gorilla gorilla* has only very sparse hair on its brows. The morphology (form, structure) of the nostrils is also different between these two gorillas: *Gorilla gorilla gorilla* has rounded nostrils, but *Gorilla gorilla beringei* has angular nostrils. Even the lips are different, for while *Gorilla gorilla gorilla* has strong lip padding, its relative has only weak lip padding.[32]

Perhaps most instructive for us amongst primate differences is the variation encountered in our closest relatives (so we are constantly being told): the chimpanzees. The physical differences between the two chimp species *Pan troglodytes verus* and *Pan paniscus* are striking. The female of *Pan troglodytes verus* possesses a white chin beard which is thick, full and rounded, but *Pan paniscus*, in contrast, has only a few beard hairs. The shape of the head is different too, for *Pan troglodytes verus* displays a broad, flat-topped head, whereas *Pan paniscus* possesses a very rounded head. The muzzle evinces marked variation also, since *Pan troglodytes verus* is typified by a broad nose and mouth, but *Pan paniscus* has a decidedly narrow muzzle. If we care to venture lower down to the anus of these two chimpanzees, we shall find that even here variation expresses itself: amongst *Pan troglodytes verus* only the young chimps have a white anal tuft, but this feature is present in most of the adults of *Pan paniscus*.

Gay apes and gay disco mice!

Since we are entering rather intimate areas, this may be the appropriate time to consider the sexual practices of the two kinds of chimpanzee: *Pan troglodytes verus* has not been noted to indulge heavily in homosexual practices, but homosexuality is frequently encountered amongst the chimpanzees of *Pan paniscus*. What does this tell us about humans? Perhaps that people with very rounded heads and a narrow mouth are more likely to be gay than persons with a broad, flattish head and a large mouth (like the chimps)? I am sure the vivisectors will try to torture some irrelevant secret out of the two types of chimpanzee.

Maybe it is indelicate of us to dwell too long in the chimps' bedroom, as it were, so we might move on (temporarily) to some less erotic details of difference. The temperament of *Pan troglodytes verus*, for example, is placid (in chimpanzee terms!), but the chimps of *Pan paniscus* are much more tense and nervous (doubtless the foolish vivisectors would say that they are neurotic and unstable, because of their predilection for gay sex. After all, some vivisectors have even claimed that disco music makes mice homosexual![33] Again, vivisectors, wedded to a reductionist, mechanistic vision of life, fail to appreciate the natural diversity of *humankind*, independently of what happens in animals — with or without disco music!).

Divergent chimp behaviour

The males of *Pan troglodytes verus* are very dominant creatures, whereas those of *Pan paniscus* are not, or only weakly so. Commenting on the two types of chimp in the prestigious scientific journal *Nature* (7.11.96, p.35), Adrienne L. Zihlman states: '... in their social behaviour, *P. paniscus* in many ways is the opposite to *P. troglodytes*'. Reviewing a major book on apes and violence, Zihlman reveals how the males of *Pan troglodytes* are '... guilty of acting abominably towards members of the same species... Males form coalitions to raid and murder their neighbours; males rape and batter females and kill their infants'. (Ibid). The males of *Pan paniscus*, in contrast, are more peaceable. Zihlman writes:

'In *P. paniscus* there is little aggression between males; males tend to ... stay close to their mothers. Males do not dominate females, and relationships between males and females are congenial and highly sexual; encounters between communities are generally friendly.

... *P. paniscus* is highly specialized anatomically, as shown by their smaller shoulder blade. The authors emphasize similarities in anatomy and behaviour between *P. troglodytes* and gorillas. But genetically the two species are much closer to each other than to any other primate, and both species are equally distant from *Homo sapiens*'. (Ibid).

The chimpanzees of *Pan troglodytes verus* are very good at 'brachiation' (swinging through the trees using their arms), but *Pan paniscus* chimpanzees seem less willing or able to indulge in this particular practice. A final amusing difference consists in the types of loud call which the two chimps emit: the apes of *Pan troglodytes verus* like to cry out 'Hoo-hoo-hoo', but the *Pan paniscus* chimps prefer to laugh out 'Hi-hi-hi'![34] What both kinds of chimpanzee scream out when they fall into the hands of the vivisectors I hate to think.

Apes in research

Touching upon the morality of using apes in 'research', Dr. R. N. Short, a pro-vivisection physiologist, has some interesting comments to make. He says that the well-being and future fertility of the great apes must be safeguarded, and that they should be protected from '… the thoughtless demands and irrelevant curiosity of scientists'.[35] Yes, thoughtless demands and irrelevant curiosity indeed, since no matter how 'similar' to us, apes are still not human, there are still unpredictable differences, which render medical tests upon them for human health research ultimately meaningless. Even if the claim that chimps are 98% genetically analogous to us is true, then one is struck by the enormity of the differences between them and us. Chimps are not, to the best of my knowledge, engaged upon the composing of symphonies, the imagining forth of Shakespeare's *The Tempest*, the elaboration of science or the constructing of pyramids or the Taj Mahal! What a colossal difference just 2% of genetic variation makes… Professor Vernon Reynolds, primatologist and Professor of Biological Anthropology at the University of Oxford, with a particular research interest in chimpanzees, states unequivocally:

> '2% genetic variation is quite a lot. There are many known genetic differences between chimps and humans. Certainly there are enough differences to make the use of chimps for medical experiments *as if they were human* NONSENSICAL'. (Letter to the author, 29.2.96.)

Elsewhere (in his Foreword to the author's booklet, *The Wrong Path*, 1996), Professor Reynolds further insists that no chimps '… *have been of any use in the experiments they were used for*, and now no one knows what to do with them'. What an appalling state of affairs. The driving force behind it all, of course, is money. As Professor Reynolds rightly points out in connection with vivisection in general and the need for its abolition: '… the whole wretched business (and it is *big* business) should be *stopped* and *stopped now*'. (Ibid.). These are the considered views of a serious, respected Oxford scientific scholar and they are views shared by many academics around the world.

Anatomical differences between apes and humans

Let us stay with chimpanzees a while longer, but now bring humans back into the frame for purposes of specific comparison. Looking at the respective anatomies of human beings and chimps we note that in humans the kidney constitutes 0.47-0.53% of total body weight, whereas in chimpanzees the kidney makes up just 0.27% of their total body weight. The shape of the gall-bladder is different in chimps and humans, for the chimp bladder has a clear bend in it, but our gall-bladder is bent only slightly. Returning to the sexual domain, we find that the testes of humans constitute 0.080% of body weight, whereas in the chimp the figure is 0.270%. The erect penis of a human male is around 130 mm in length (give or take a little), but the chimp is rather less well endowed, with a penis length of just 80 mm. The flaccid (non-erect) penis in man is pendulous (it dangles), but it is withdrawn in the case of the chimp. The breast development of human females is permanent, but is only evident in chimpanzees during lactation. Turning to the skin glands, we find that humans have no apocrine glands on the torso — only under the armpits and on the groins — whereas chimps do possess some, and orangs and certain other species of monkey possess many; furthermore, the apocrine orifices are well inside human skin, but near the surface of chimpanzee skin. The sebaceous glands of humans are well developed, but display only meagre development in chimpanzees, just as in this connection the human is rich in the body-chemical, glycogen, but chimpanzees possess but little of it.

If we look at hair growth, we discover that the number of hairs on the scalp per cm^2 is only 188 in chimpanzees, but humans have around 300 hairs per square cm of scalp (some of us, unfortunately, have far fewer!); on the chest, however, the situation is reversed, with chimps putting forth a generous 70 hairs per cm^2 but humans having a paltry 1 hair per cm^2 only.[36]

If we compare the arms of humans and monkeys generally, we encounter definite differences in musculature and function: the monkey arm '... scrves a locomotor function in addition to a reaching function. This is reflected in the structures of the spine and shoulder'.[37] Those structures are, needless to say, different from the human. And lastly there are distinct differences regarding muscle morphology and 'insertion' (i.e. the point where the muscle attaches to the bone) not only between humans and apes, but amongst monkeys and apes themselves. If we take the deltoid muscle of the arm, we will see that the '... morphology of the deltoid is very different within primates. In quadrupeds, the muscle is not very well developed. In the so-called semibrachiators, the deltoid is more fully developed than in quadrupeds, but a slight reduction of the spinal and clavicular portions is present …'[38] What all this means is simply that different types of primate have different forms and positionings of the deltoid muscle. A similar situation obtains regarding the latissimus dorsi muscle in the arm: 'There are three different types of insertion in simians'[39] (i.e. apes and monkeys). Comparing the species *Cercopithecus aethiops* and *Cercopithecus sabaeus*, Dr. Michael Schultz expresses surprise over the difference of 'insertion' found in the latissimus dorsi of these two monkeys: 'It is striking', he says, 'that *closely related* species like *Cercopithecus aethiops* and *Cercopithecus sabaeus* have *such a different type* of insertion'.[40] (Emphasis added). The chest (pectoral) muscles are also variable between monkeys, apes and men.[41] Lastly, the panniculus carnosus (a thin sheet of muscle which serves to produce local movement of the skin)

> '… is very variable in primates. In Tupaia, this muscle represents a well-developed muscular layer. In the platyrrhines, the muscle is distinctly reduced or even missing. The panniculus carnosus in Cercopithecidae is relatively well developed, whereas the muscle is generally missing in apes'.[42]

These are just a few of the many differences between monkeys, apes and humans. As Drs. H. Steklis and J. Erwin observe: 'The range of variation in structure and function of primate biological and behavioral systems is *dramatic*' (emphasis added). We must not forget here that the category 'primate' includes human beings, so what the above statement clearly reveals is that humans and monkeys display enormous differences, one from the other, as Professor Vernon Reynolds earlier indicated.

Skin differences between animals and humans

If humans and our nearest relatives are so different, we might expect the variations between ourselves and non-primate species (rats, mice, cats, dogs, etc.) to be even more pronounced — and we would be right. Let us return to an area touched upon a few lines back — that of the skin, its glands and hair.

The sebaceous glands are glands located in the skin which secrete an oily substance called sebum that slowly and constantly flows out onto the skin itself. In humans sebum is made up of approximately 40% triglycerides, 28% free fatty acids, 17% hydrocarbons, 10% higher fatty alcohols and 5% cholesterol. Yet if we compare human sebum with that of animals, we discover that '… man is *unique* in producing a surface lipid which consists predominantly of triglycerides and their breakdown products (di- and mono-glycerides and fatty acids)'.[43] (Emphasis added). Human skin differs considerably, in fact, from animal skin, particularly in the following ways:

a) the sebaceous glands are of a different size

b) the sebaceous gland cycle is different

c) the sweat glands are of a different type, and are distributed differently
and with a variant frequency

d) the chemical and enzymatic constituents of human skin are different

e) the response to vitamins, steroids and irritants is different

f) the number of hairs per given area and their growth cycle are different.[44]

In humans, there are, as we indicated earlier, something like 40-70 hairs per cm^2 of body-surface area, but in most other mammals (and humans are mammals too, we must remember) the ratio is much higher — around 4,000 hairs/cm^2 for rats and mice, for example.

Vivisectors like to do experiments to see how rapidly various chemicals that come into contact with the skin get absorbed into it. But using animal skin (sometime stripped off the animal) for this purpose is of course misleading due to the above-mentioned differences. Drs. Katz and Poulsen (themselves vivisectionists) actually express the view that it seems pointless '... to further *complicate* the research problems by the use of *animal* skin, *animal* membranes, such as sheeps (sic!) bladder ...'[45] (emphasis added), when human skin, available from cadavers for instance, would be far more relevant. Commenting on the many efforts that have been made to develop animal 'models' for assessing chemical absorption through the skin (in an attempt to mimic what happens in human skin), Drs. Katz and Poulsen have published the following revealing remarks:

> 'Many efforts have been made to develop laboratory animal models in which the rates and routes of percutaneous absorption would *approximate* those of man. *This goal has seldom been achieved*, since humans and animals display *wide differences in the physical characteristics of their skin*, such as the number of appendageal openings per unit area and the thickness of the stratum corneum. These physical and structural differences obviously affect the penetration pathways and the penetration resistance of skin. *Furthermore, biochemical differences between animal and human skin, even when subtle, may significantly alter skin reactions with penetrant chemicals*'.[46] (Emphasis added)

This is a key point for us to grasp: in trying to transfer data from an animal to a human, even the most minute of differences can upset the experiment and render it invalid. And since one never knows all the variables between animals and humans in advance when testing a new chemical or procedure, one never knows how and when the animal is going to 'trip one up' in one's foolhardy attempts at extrapolation. What is found in an animal in no way represents a promise that the same will be found in a human — so *guessing* becomes the order of the day (as we shall hear a vivisector confess in Chapter Six).

To illustrate the variations in the absorptive response as between the skin of animals and humans, we should like to cite what happened when various chemicals, chemical warfare agents and other chemical agent stimulants were applied to the skin of various animals. It was found by the experimenters that the back skin of weanling pigs most closely *approximated* human forearm skin with regard to its resistance to penetration. But the forearm of the chimpanzee (our 'closest relative') was actually less permeable than that of humans. In contrast, the back skins of monkey, dog, cat, horse, rabbit, goat, guinea-pig and mouse were, in that order, increasingly more permeable than the forearm skin of humans. Additive substances which facilitated or enhanced penetration of an agent through the highly permeable mouse skin were found to be noticeably less effective in rabbit skin, and still less in human skin.[47] Other researchers found that the skins of rats and cynomolgus monkeys were *over 50 times* more permeable than human skin to the corticosteroid, diflorasone diacetate, whereas hairless mouse skin revealed similar permeability to human skin for three steroids and the n-alkanols, but was approximately *1,000 times more permeable than human skin* for the chemical, paraquat (*Pharmacology of the Skin II*, ed. Greaves and Shuster, Springer-Verlag, 1989, p.105). What all this Tower of Babel of inconsistent, confusing data proves is anybody's guess — except that one can never know which animal's skin is a dependable dermatological model for the human being. It is all hit and miss — not worthy of the name science (which in Latin means knowledge).

The same uselessness of vivisection in connection with skin diseases is also worth contemplating. First of all, vivisectors admit that it is 'difficult' (to say the least) to produce in animals diseased skin states that have '... any close similarity or correlation to those found in man'.[48] Sound familiar? Failing to create the actual human skin disease, the vivisectors then compound their error and folly by trying out drugs on the artificially skin-damaged animals, who will not reliably respond in the same way as humans, even if they were suffering from the same disease (which of course they are not). Drs. Katz and Poulsen rightly point out:

'The response of these *simulated* cutaneous disorders to drugs can be *misleading,* and data obtained from such experimental models are *never unqualifiedly applicable to man'.*[49] (Emphasis added).

They surely are not! And it is not only in the area of drug responses that animals vary from humans, but even in such basic functions as their capacity for smell, taste and hearing, etc. We might in fact pause here for a moment over these differences in the sensory processing mechanisms displayed by animals.

Differences in animal and human 'senses'

A most important fact to grasp from the outset is that the sensory receptors of the various animals are specialised for each animal species, to match their life-style, food preferences, visual and auditory environments, etc.[50] One of the very oldest senses of which animals and humans are possessed is that of smell (the olfactory system), but even here there are differences. Many animals have a far more developed sense of smell than us humans, and even differ amongst themselves. Smelling a substance is a function of breathing (we cannot smell anything if we do not breathe; of course, if we do not breathe, we will not live to do anything else anyway). As we breathe, olfactory stimuli are drawn across the olfactory receptor sheet, or 'olfactory epithelium' (i.e. the tissue that covers the surface of the vital odour-responsive part of our sensory equipment), which is located down in the airway and is highly convoluted in mammals. What is of interest for our purposes is that the receptive surface area of this epithelium *varies greatly from species to species*, from 100 cm^2 in dogs to only a few square centimetres in humans.[51]

Now when we come to the sense of taste (itself connected to that of smell) we find even more startling differences. Vivisectors generally assume that laboratory animals have four basic taste sensations, but human beings are known to have far more, plus the fact that '... experimental animals are widely divergent in their [taste-mechanism] sensitivity to chemical compounds'.[52] The vivisector, James C. Boudreau, wanted to compare the biochemistry and neurology involved in the taste-response of various animals to different substances. He commenced with the cat, and then moved on to other creatures. Surprise, surprise! There were differences. The dog, for example (which is a carnivore 'closely related' to the cat) displayed neurons involved in the tasting process which could be divided into three neural groups, but only *one* of those groups seemed (even this was not certain) identical to the corresponding group found in the cat. The amino acid group of the dog responded well to the amino acids that were stimulatory in the cat, but it also responded to some amino acids that were *not* excitatory in the cat and to sugars, *which were completely inactive in the cat*.[53] The pig also displays differences: at least four neural groups have been identified in the pig in the tasting process, and it seems that two of them *are different from those present in other species*.[54]

We mentioned earlier that humans have more than just four tastes. Food chemists have discovered that we have at least 13 taste sensations that have a certain amount of 'psychophysics' and chemistry involved in them. What is clear is that (as with virtually everything else) humans have a different set of taste responses from animals. Even the vivisector, James C. Boudreau, is forced to recognise this uniqueness of the human being. He writes:

'In attempting to match mammalian neural groups with human taste sensations, one discovers that the human taste system is *far more complex than that of any of the animals studied*. Furthermore, no one animal *approximates* the human: rather a composite of systems from different species is required to make *even a rough* match. Also, *for some human sensations no adequate animal analogs exist, nor does there seem to be a human equivalent for some animal systems*'.[55] (Emphasis added.)

No excitatory analogue of the 'bitter' sensation is present in any experimental animal, nor is the human taste sensation, known by the Japanese term, umami-1, found in the neurophysiology of other mammals. And in case the reader is wondering whether the closeness of taste sensations to those of the human cannot perhaps be gauged by the position of the animal in the scale of evolution (the phylogenetic chain), we might add, to confound any such optimistic belief, that the lobster seems to have as many (or as few) taste systems in common with the human as the goat does![56]

Finally (in this section on the senses), even the auditory (hearing) ability is of course different across the species. Vivisectors are particularly fond of 'studying' the hearing of cats and primates and trying (always futilely) to equate them with the human mechanisms. But even here the vivisectors themselves admit that identicalness is not to be found. After mentioning bats, the vivisector Dennis P. Phillips proceeds to speak of cats and primates:

'A fortuitous feature of the auditory behavioural capacities of these animals is that, *in some respects*, they parallel those of the human'.[57] (Emphasis added.)

If something resembles another thing 'in some respects' only, it is not calculated to be a very reliable general guide. Phillips seems to recognise this fact when immediately after the above-quoted statement he adds the caveat: 'It may be optimistic to expect these similarities to extend to the underlying neural mechanisms ...'[58]

The vivisectors know that difference is the rule at the microscopic level rather than identity — but they remain 'optimistic' and press on with their methodologically flawed work.

❀ ❀

Back to the monkeys

Let us end this chapter where we began it — with the primates. If we compare the proportion of surface area occupied by the 'frontal region' of the brain in humans and monkeys, we find that whereas in humans the proportion of that frontal area to the total cortical surface is 29.0%, it is only 16.9% in chimpanzees (*Pan troglodytes*), 9.5% in baboons (*Papio hamadryas*), 9.2% in Capuchin monkeys (*Cebus capucinus*) and 8.9% in the black-pencilled marmoset (*Callithrix penicillata*). In dogs we might add it is only 6.9% and in cats a mere 3.4%. Rabbits have an even smaller frontal region to their brain than cats — in them it occupies only 2.2% of the total cortical surface area.[59]

The structure of the brain is a particularly fascinating area of divergence as between humans and other animals, since the variations are so telling. The evolution of the human brain is not simply a case of its 'adding on' completely new 'bits', but of its elaborating trends already found in other species. As an instance of this, we could cite the case of the superior temporal gyrus (a raised convolution of the cerebral cortex) in both humans and rhesus monkeys: the human equivalent of the area of the superior temporal gyrus known as 'paAlt' in the rhesus monkey differentiates into two subdivisions in people, called areas 'paAi' and 'paAe'.[60] The primary sensory cortices of the human are also very different, in terms of cell architecture, from those of the rhesus monkey.[61]

The area of the brain called the prefrontal cortex yields valuable fruit for us, since not only does its relative size vary between species, but even its position within the brain; in fact, the prefrontal cortex can differ 'quite considerably'[62] between individual members of the very same species.

The thalamus (a kind of relay station for messages to the brain) has been studied for decades, particularly in tree shrews and primates, and yet all attempts at equating the thalamic nuclei of primates and other mammals — or even homologising between primates and primates — are still '... far from satisfactory because of *variations* in thalamic structure'.[63] (Emphasis added).

When we turn to the eye and visual systems of primates, we discover significant differences there too. Unlike most other mammals, whom scientists suspect of being colour blind, primates can distinguish between colours, and their visual systems are relatively well developed at birth — much of the crucial development occurring *before* birth. Primates (distinct from many other creatures) are born with their eyes open and with at least basic visual function. Of course the visual system does not remain static, but unfolds into greater complexity as the animal approaches maturity. Yet here we come across further variation, for the time-period over which post-natal changes in the visual system take place varies in different primates with their different rates of maturation: humans and apes take many years to reach full maturity, but some monkeys, such as marmosets and prosimians in general, dash to full maturity in just one year or so.[64]

A most important requirement for being able to 'see' amongst primates is the development of the lateral geniculate nucleus (LGN), which is the primary source of input to the visual cortex. The LGN is a relay nucleus, but its neurons also modify retinal input. Now, what is so interesting is that the LGN is arranged in laminae (layers of tissue), which display '... *marked variability* in the laminar pattern across primate species'.[65] (Emphasis added). So even such a basic function as seeing is motored by neural variations within the familial ranges of primates themselves, let alone other animals. Nothing in nature is in all respects identical, exactly the same in one species as in another. It is such variety which makes our world so richly expressive, and which ensures that vivisecting animals to gain dependable knowledge about humans is doomed to failure from the very start.

While we are on the subject of vision, we might cast our own eyes upon the retinas of macaque monkeys: the retina (the light-sensitive layer of tissue that lines the interior of the eye) in macaques (and possibly other primates too) contains a ganglion cell type (biplexiform) which makes direct contact with photoreceptors. *Nothing similar has been found in any other vertebrate.* This means that the macaque retina (or primate retina, perhaps) appears *unique.*[66] Some researchers have argued that although the primate retina may indeed be unique in this sense, the ganglion cell types that comprise the major part of the thalamocortical pathway in primates (midget and parasol cells) are 'quite similar' to those that comprise the major part of this pathway in carnivores (beta and alpha cells).[67] Yet even Dr. Rodieck, a researcher prepared to entertain the notion that these various cells are homologous, admits that this is only a 'hypothesis'[68] — i.e. an unproven guess.

Things are becoming very technical, so let us move on to a simpler, but more dramatic, area of difference: namely, what happens to the behaviour of monkeys and people when the 'same' part of their brain is damaged or removed. As the reader will readily imagine, vivisectors have for innumerable decades been deliberately injuring monkeys' brains. With what results? Let us see.

The early researchers at the turn of the century who exercised themselves in damaging the prefrontal cortex of monkeys' brains frequently came up with results different from one another and could not agree as to which functions of the brain were affected by the damage inflicted upon specific areas.[69] This happens often in vivisection: different vivisectors get different results from the same experiment. On this basis alone, vivisection stands indicted of unreliability and futility. Anyhow, more recently it has been established that removing or damaging a certain segment of the 'supplementary motor area' of the brain in humans has a dramatic effect upon behaviour: the victims suffer from global bilateral akinesia (that is, a total loss of normal muscular tonicity or responsiveness) and also fall mute. The situation is decidedly different with analogously damaged monkeys: they display only minor diminution in their total functioning — a 'poverty of deficits'.[70] Similarly, disturbance to the parietal lobes of the brain in humans results in a distinctive type of behavioural effect: the human patient becomes afflicted with apraxia (the inability to make skilled movements with accuracy), whereas parietal damage in monkeys yields noticeably weaker effects, and these for only a short period of time.[71] Commenting on this, the vivisector, Dr. Hepp-Reymond, writes:

'These observations express the major quantitative and qualitative differences between nonhuman primates and man, related to the important development of the neocortex and its associative areas'.[72]

Another significant difference between monkeys and people in this area is that whereas in the macaque monkey the proportion of motor to premotor cortex surface area of the brain is 1 to 1, in humans it is 1 to 6.[72]

Vivisectors have also tried to see whether amnesia (loss of memory) is produced by damage to the limbic system (a complex of nerve pathways and networks in the brain), but as so often the vivisectors cannot agree, since they achieve different results ...[73]

Even such minor changes in behaviour as the way brain-damaged monkeys will respond to someone staring at them will vary with the species: if the orbitofrontal region of the brain is artificially damaged in vervet and rhesus monkeys, the two species react differently when stared at by a human — the vervet monkey will become more aggressive, while the rhesus monkey will become the *very opposite*.[74]

Before we close this chapter, let us return to the sex lives of monkeys and see how sex hormones affect them. When castrated male rhesus monkeys are given fairly low doses of testosterone, for example, they become more sexually active and rampant; but the *same* dose in the *same* test conditions will have *no* effect on cynomolgus macaque monkeys. Moreover, the sexual responsiveness of both male and female rhesus monkeys is able to be hormonally enhanced much more than that of stumptail macaques or lowland gorillas. But even here variation raises its ubiquitous head, for the amount of sex engaged in by rhesus monkeys, and other kinds too, will be modified by the different environments into which they are placed. Another factor which can change the results obtained is whether higher-ranking or lower-ranking monkeys are present. Dr. Eberhart, an expert in this field, comments on how species differences become apparent and are inevitable when monkeys' endocrine systems are artificially interfered with by the introduction of sex hormones:

'Given the *diversity* of social structure and ecological specializations represented by the cercopithecine primates, *such differences are not surprising.*[75] (Emphasis added)

No, such differences are not surprising, since difference is the rule rather than the exception. When will the vivisectors ever face up to this simple fact?

Further variations are encountered when vivisectors deprive monkeys of their ovaries and then attempt to restore sexual behaviour in them: in many monkeys this is successful through oestrogen replacement 'therapy', but this does *not* fully restore sexual behaviour in ovariectomised thick-tailed galagos monkeys.

Callitrichid monkeys deviate from the hormonal patterns prominent in Old World primates in that their levels of serum androstenedione and oestrone are considerably higher than are those of testosterone and oestradiol. Moreover, the reproductive potential of the common marmoset monkey is a great deal higher than that of other monkeys.[76]

Hormonal differences are in fact found in connection with the androgen hormones generally: there is considerable variability in the predominant androgens (and oestrogens too) across different species, with some androgens predominating in some primates but not in others. And of course changes in the time of year (the season) elicit different sexual responses across the range of primate species.[77]

How does all this relate to men and women? Nobody knows. Humans vary even more than monkeys. Dr. Eberhart rightly states:

'In conclusion, the *variability* in responsiveness and in experimental procedures that influence studies of nonhuman primates are present, and often *accentuated*, in studies with humans, *making generalization difficult*'.[78] (Emphasis added)

Yes, that is precisely the point: vivisectors are forever trying to make sweeping generalisations from data which are simply too disparate and chaotic to be welded into one meaningful whole. It is time the experimenters stopped attempting to 'homologise' animals and humans; it is time they stopped indulging in the grossest forms of anthropomorphism science has ever seen. It is time they learned life's constant lesson: nature's creations are unique and individual.

CHAPTER FOUR

Of Rats, Mice, Dogs and Humans

Undoubtedly the experimenters' favourite (but, as we have already seen, by no means exclusively used) laboratory animals are mice and rats. All over the world these creatures are dragooned into countless experiments. One would expect, therefore, that there must be some overriding *scientific* reason as to why these little rodents are chosen. Do they, for instance, possess physiological, metabolic and immunological processes which are uniquely close to human ones? Are they anatomically the same as us? Are they characterised by acts of mentation which are all exactly the same as our own? Do they possess the same social structures and interactions as ourselves? The answer to all these questions is an emphatic *'No!'* Then why are they so widely used?

We shall find the answer in a major monograph on the subject of the laboratory rat, a book compiled by two vivisectors (so presumably they know what they are speaking about). This is what they write:

'The albino rat has come to be the most widely used laboratory animal. This extensive use is due to a number of factors such as *low cost, small space requirement, tractability* [i.e. docile and malleable nature], omnivorous dietary, short time span of generations, *large litters* and the fact that the rat can be readily standardized ...

As has been pointed out, rats are *less expensive* than large animals to buy and maintain, their living quarters require *less space*, and consequently *more animals may be used*. The animals themselves are *easier to handle* ...'[79] (Emphasis added)

So it becomes clear from this that chief among the highly scholarly and scientific reasons why rats are so widely used is because they are cheap, small, and easy to pick up!

At this point the reader might interject: 'But the vivisectors here are talking about *bonus* reasons for using these animals'. Sadly, this is not the case. Professor Croce, himself a vivisector for many years, has stated in his excellent, ground-breaking book, *Vivisection or Science: A Choice to Make*, that rodents are used primarily because they are relatively cheap, small and not inclined to bite too much. Another vivisector, the Nobel Laureate Dr. Alexis Carrel, who spent decades vivisecting animals, including at the Rockefeller Institute for Medical Research, stated unequivocally that mice and rats have '... only *very remote* analogies with man'[80] (emphasis added), and in 1996 the vivisector, Professor Ed Masoro, confirmed regarding rat experiments that '... there is no reason to believe that what is true for rats will necessarily be true for human beings' (*Daily Mail,* 29.1.96). So there can be no serious suggestion that these animals are used because they are physiologically close to us. They are not. The fact is that it is *convenient* to use rodents, nothing more. No wonder that when vivisection avails itself so extensively of creatures physically 'very remote' from us when testing drugs, etc. we end up with so much pharmacological damage being engendered in human patients — the *real* 'guinea-pigs' (see Chapter Eight).

Rodents are not humans

It will be something of an eye-opener, I believe, to learn of some of the differences between rodents (rats and mice) and humans. Here is a selective list:

1 Plaque (a fatty substance) is deposited in the liver of rodents but in the blood vessels of humans (leading to stroke and heart disease).

2 Laboratory rodents live only about 3 years, and are given massive doses of test chemicals, whereas humans live 70 or 80+ years and consume such chemicals in minute doses over a much longer time-scale.

3 Imuran (an immunosuppressive drug) causes birth defects in mice, but not in humans.

4 Rats and mice (along with cats, dogs and hamsters) synthesize Vitamin C in their own bodies (as we noted earlier), whereas humans require Vitamin C in their diets, if they are not to die of scurvy.

5 Lysodren (a cancer chemotherapy drug) does not cause kidney damage in rodents, but it does cause kidney damage in people.

6 Continual pregnancy is healthy for rodents, but in women it leads to nutritional depletion and disease.

7 Rats and mice are hypersensitive to chlorine in minute doses, whereas humans can tolerate chlorine in much larger doses (witness municipal swimming-pools).

8 Myambutol (a TB antibiotic) causes birth defects in mice, but not in humans.

9   Rats and mice process Vitamin B in their appendix, but humans store it in their liver.

10 Certain drugs which rodents can eliminate from their body in about 3 hours (thus reducing the risk of dangerous toxicity) can take up to 72 hours to be eliminated in humans.

11 Thymidine shrinks tumours in mice, but not in humans.

12 Catapress (clonidine) is a drug for high blood-pressure which causes retinal damage in rats, but not in the human retina.

13 Rats and mice cannot comfortably tolerate more than about 15 minutes of direct sunlight, whereas we humans like to lap up the sunshine as though there were no tomorrow!

14 Chloroform is toxic to mice in minute doses, but humans can stand it in much larger amounts.

15 Mice and rats obtain Vitamin D by licking their own fur, whereas we obtain it from our diet and from sunshine.

16 Moban (a tranquillizer) causes breast tumours in mice, but not in humans.

17 Rodents are specially bred for laboratory studies. They live in a sterile, controlled environment. Most of the ailments they are made to suffer from in the laboratory are artificially created. Humans, on the other hand, come from a rich variety of uncontrolled, un sterilised environments and develop disease spontaneously.

18 Rats have no gall bladder and digest fats differently from humans. Humans have a gall bladder.

19 Rats and mice require 3 1/2 times more protein (relative to size) than humans. Excess protein in humans is responsible for kidney damage.

20 Meclazine (for travel sickness) causes birth defects in rats, but not in humans.

21 Coumarin (a blood thinner) causes liver damage in rodents, but not in humans.

22 Rats, mice (and rabbits too) have no vomiting reflex, whereas we humans can vomit (for example, if we witness the folly and cruelty of a vivisection experiment!)[81]

Nor are dogs!

We could extend the above list almost indefinitely, but let us do a similar exercise with dogs (also quite popular as lab animals). Here are some of the important differences:

1 Oral contraceptives prolong blood-clotting time in dogs, but can increase the risk of fatal blood clots in women (in 1995, for instance, there was a big scare over certain brands of The Pill, which were found to double the risk of thromboses in women).

2 Chloramphenicol does not cause the fatal blood disease, aplastic anaemia, in dogs (instead, just a transient anaemia), but chloramphenicol can cause aplastic anaemia in people.

3 Dogs, as we have already seen, require no Vitamin C in their diet, but dietary Vitamin C is essential to humans.

4 The anti-cancer drug, Azauridine, causes fatal bone marrow depression in dogs after only 7-10 days, but is tolerated for comparatively long periods by people.

5 Aspirin causes birth defects in dogs, but not in normal doses in humans.

6 The arthritis drug, Ibufenac, does not cause liver damage in dogs, but does in people.

7 The anti-cancer drug, Mitoxantrone, does not affect dogs' hearts, but it has caused heart failure in people.

8 The body chemical, acetylcholine, dilates dogs' coronary arteries, but constricts human coronary arteries, leading to heart spasms.

9 Relatively high doses of isoprenaline are safe for dogs, but much smaller doses (in aerosol inhalers) proved deadly for asthmatic humans, killing an estimated 3,500 in Britain alone in the 1960s.

10 The arthritis drug, Fenclozic acid, does not damage dogs' livers, but has caused liver toxicity in people.

11 Digitalis for treating cardiopathies raises the blood pressure in dogs, but lowers it in humans ...[82]

It would be quite possible to go through every laboratory animal and highlight crucial differences between them and us — but perhaps we should return to our friends, the rodents, as well as calling in upon some other creatures along the way, to see just how inexact and open to all manner of result-changing circumstances vivisection can be.

Confounding variables in animal experimentation

Professor Floyd R. Domer, a vivisector at Tulane University, New Orleans during the 1970s, wrote a revealing book on the use of animals in pharmacological analysis, from which we should like to quote numerous examples of how seemingly small variables can radically alter the outcome of an animal experiment.

'*It is not uncommon for an investigator to find that he is unable to reproduce results which have been reported from another laboratory*' (emphasis added), writes Professor Domer,[83] and therewith puts his finger on just how unreliable vivisection really is. One of the reasons for this frequent divergence of results is that the environment of the lab animals can vary and exert different effects upon the different animals. One such variable is that of — bedding! Yes, the straw or other material placed in the animals' cages. It was found that mice that had been bedded down on red cedar chips reacted differently to the soporific effects of sodium hexobarbital and sodium pentobarbital from those mice which had been housed on ground corncob bedding. The first group of mice slept 50% less than the other group, despite being given the same dosage of sleeping drug.[84]

Another variable which can radically alter the physiology of test animals is environmental stress. A team of vivisectors found that profound physiological and tissue changes emerged in young rats who were kept in isolated conditions for several months. The effect of this unnatural situation was that the rats suffered a decrease in cardiac potassium and magnesium levels and a marked increase in heart sodium and calcium levels. As regards tissue, there was a striking tendency towards haemorrhage and necrosis (the death of some or all cells of an organ or tissue). When the rats were returned to the company of other rats, they reverted to normal, fairly rapidly.[85]

Noise is another factor that can alter the effects of an experiment. A vivisector in the 1940s found that applying external noise to groups of mice kept in a jar greatly increased the harmful effects of sympathomimetic amines upon those mice. He also found that contrary to what we might have expected from the isolation-and-stress experimental results mentioned above, aggregation (i.e. bringing lots of creatures together in a confined space) also significantly *increased* the toxicity of the same chemicals in mice.

That particular vivisector also noticed that the *temperature* of the lab affected the outcome of experiments with mice, since an increase in room temperature from 60° to 80°F rendered the mice more susceptible to the toxic effects of sympathomimetic amines — and this to an equal extent, regardless of whether the animals were in solitary confinement or in groups![86]

Another vivisector found that *lowering* the animals' environmental temperature caused rats which had been given reserpine to develop more gastric ulcers than those rats kept warmer.[87] So it seems the vivisectors cannot win: if a certain temperature prevails on one day they will get one set of results, and a different set of results when the temperature changes a few days later. What kind of 'science' is that? And we, the public, are expected to put our faith and trust in the reliability and efficacy of such 'safety' tests for our cosmetics and medicines! Even Shakespeare knew better (see Chapter Ten).

Of course diet is another important factor in determining the outcome of an experiment. The amount and nature of the food given to an animal will affect its health and its urinary excretory patterns, for example, and alter the pH of its urine.[88] This can lead to misleading results in some types of experiment. And of course a diet that is bad for laboratory animals may well be very good for us humans — or vice versa.

Even the solvent in which a drug is administered can alter the onset, intensity and duration of that drug's action upon a lab animal. The vivisector, Coldman, found that the introduction of a volatile solvent, isopropanol, to a mixture of chemicals increased the skin-penetrative power of an anti-inflammatory steroid applied to the unbroken skin.[89] Use of the solvent, dimethylsulfoxide (DMSO), can increase the toxicity of a larger number of quaternary ammonium compounds in mice and rats.[90]

Profound differences in experimental result can also be elicited by the *route* of drug administration, i.e. whether it is given orally or injected into the animal in some other way. For example, botulinal toxin will kill rabbits in just 2 hours 25 minutes if it is injected intravenously, but it will take *4 days 9 hours* to kill them if it is administered via the rectum![91]

Anaesthetics in animals

Anaesthetics can also have significant effects upon animals, effects which can muddle the data supplied by an experiment. Dogs anaesthetised, for example, with a mixture of chloralose and urethane undergo a steady decrease in cardiovascular function as the anaesthetics take greater hold. This kind of physiological alteration will change the response of those dogs to drugs which act upon the cardiovascular system.[92]

One of the most extraordinary facts about the use of anaesthetics in laboratory animals is that the back-to-front vivisectors, instead of basing themselves on animal data, attempt to assess the anaesthetic depth arrived at in their lab animals by *extrapolating from the human classification of depth and human reflex actions*. In other words, vivisectors when trying to investigate humans try to transfer results from animals to people, but when dealing with anaesthesia in *animals* they do the reverse and extrapolate from *humans* to animals! Moreover, the vivisectors have scant regard for the wellbeing of the animals they are anaesthetising. According to the specialist journal, *Laboratory Animals* (Vol. 26, No. 3, July 1992, p.159), some vivisectors regard the loss of 9% of their animal charges through anaesthetic complications as 'low'. No wonder that '... reliable data concerning the mortality associated with commonly used anaesthetics in laboratory species are not available ...' (ibid). It would seem that even the vivisectors are embarrassed to publish statistics on the animal deaths they have caused by wrongly applied anaesthetics alone. *Lab Animals* actually entertains the possibility that:

> '... we [i.e. vivisectors] are over-anaesthetizing laboratory animals, and ... are guilty of insufficient physiological monitoring, and that this is having a detrimental effect on the well-being of the animals, and possibly *the validity of the experimental results which are obtained*'. (Ibid, emphasis added).

So even before the experiment has begun, and independently of the variations as between humans and animals, the experiment is admitted by vivisectors themselves as possibly being invalid because of the manner in which the anaesthetics are administered. Speaking of species variation, *Lab Animals* discloses that amongst animals '...there is a *wide variation* in response to a drug, so the administration of a single bolus [i.e. a large pharmaceutical preparation or pill] will inevitably be overdosing many of the animals. If the anaesthetic agent has a narrow safety margin, then this will result in the *deaths of many animals*, and an *unnecessarily severe challenge to many more*'. (Ibid., emphasis added). The vivisectors are not quite sure how deeply anaesthetized an animal might be, since there is so much individual variation. One researcher in 1988 succeeded in killing *five out of six* rabbits by wrongly administering the anaesthetic, pentobarbitone, and drawing the wrong conclusions from the rabbits' foot reflexes (ibid.). That vivisector discovered that it was not possible *to extrapolate from one part of an animal to another body-part regarding anaesthetic depth, since the front-leg reflexes disappeared at a different level of anaesthesia from the reflexes of the hind-legs!* (Ibid.). And the vivisectors would have us believe that they can reliably extrapolate from animal-test results to human beings. The impossibility of this will be obvious to the commonsense of the logical and intelligent reader.

Age, weight and amphetamines

Returning to the numerous variables that can alter a vivisection outcome: weight is yet another factor which can change the result of an animal experiment. This is particularly crucial when we remember that the dosages of human medicines are largely based upon the dose/response ratio of a test animal *according to body weight*. But as Professor Domer points out in connection with trying to standardize drug quantities given to lab animals:

> 'This approach is based on the assumption that there is a uniform distribution of the drug throughout the body. However, there are many studies to show that blood distribution, total metabolic activity and many other factors vary greatly from tissue to tissue.[93]

Age, too, is enormously important, as it can completely reverse the effects obtained from a drug or procedure performed upon different animals. Newborn animals display very different responses to chemicals and other stimuli from older animals. For example, rats, hamsters, rabbits and mice are born with functionally underdeveloped blood-brain barriers and have brain amine levels much lower than their adult equivalents. The newborn of these species do not suffer seizures when given lethal doses of paralytic shellfish poison, whereas newborn guinea-pigs and chicks are born with functionally mature brains and they convulse before dying following the administration of lethal doses of shellfish poison. The brain amine concentrations of newborn guinea-pigs are essentially the same as those found in adult guinea-pigs, whereas chicks have higher concentrations of norepinephrine and lower concentrations of 5-hydroxytryptamine than adult chickens.[94]

A striking difference in drug toxicity can be called forth by giving amphetamine to young and adult mice: in one experiment it was found that the amphetamine did not become more toxic to the young mice when they were placed in groups in a cage, but it became much more poisonous to adult mice when they were placed in groups in a cage.[95] What does this tell us about humans? Not to put adults into a cage with other adults after dosing them up with amphetamines, perhaps?

Regarding age differences, for years now surgeons have assumed that the hearts of newborn human babies are more resistant to the effects of cardiac surgery than are those of adults — despite the fact that postoperative low-output syndrome and deaths are much higher amongst newborn babies than adults after heart surgery. *The Lancet* (16 November 1996, p.1325) interestingly points out that this belief in the greater resilience of the newborn's heart is a '... *prejudice* based upon a substantial body of research done in *animal models*' (emphases added), and that this animal-based prejudice is now being challenged by the findings in humans of Dr. D.P. Taggart and colleagues (*Heart*, 1996; 76: pp.215-217). Once again, vivisection would appear to have been pointing modern medicine in the dangerously wrong direction.

Impossibility of reliable extrapolation across species boundaries

Of course the type of animal (the particular species) used in vivisection will largely determine the results the experimenter gets. This whole book is full of examples of these species differences. Perhaps we might mention a further couple of striking instances of species variation here:

When an analgesic (pain-killer) was given to rabbits and rats, it was discovered that they were unaffected by as much as 80 or 100 mg/kg/day respectively; yet when the same analgesic was administered to dogs and monkeys, it was found that more than 30 mg/kg/day caused vomiting, weight loss, depression, unconsciousness and occasionally even death![96] How would *you* guess the right dose for humans? Or would you even want to give it to humans at all? Your guess is as good as the vivisectors'!

The chemical, isoproterenol, *lowers* the blood pressure in some animals — but in rabbits, it slightly *increases* it![97]

What would *you* do faced with this difference? Would you feel there is safety in numbers, or would you feel that the rabbit just might be similar to the human in its reaction to this substance? Nobody can tell.

It is because of all these variations in animal responses that many investigators (e.g. Litchfield, Zbinden, Carr, Croce) have questioned, or denied outright, the validity of using animals to determine drug actions in humans. Professor Domer adds his own doubts when he states:

'There has been no satisfactory conclusion reached on the dilemma as to what extent investigators may rely upon the use of animals for investigation of drug actions and the predictability of drug actions in animals for their usefulness in man'.[98]

One of the reasons why extrapolation of animal data to human beings is practically impossible is the different rates of drug metabolism effected in different species. We shall just briefly note the case of the chemical, meperidine, in this regard: meperidine is metabolised in humans at a rate of roughly 17% per hour, whereas a dog will metabolise it at a rate of up to 90% per hour![99]

Professor Domer is all too aware of these confounding variables (which also include the effects of handling an animal, seasonal effects, influence of

light and darkness, and genetic differences found even within the same strain
of animals from different breeders). Domer adds further worry into the whole
scenario when he admits:

> 'Additionally, it is likely that there are as many, *or many more*, factors
> which have not yet been clarified and which may have an effect upon the
> response obtained following the administration of a compound to a
> biological system'.[100] (Emphasis added)

It is all of these factors, known and unknown, which cause Professor
Domer, himself an active vivisector, to sum up in the following words:

> 'Differences in the metabolism of compounds by each species makes
> this type of extrapolation a *hazardous* procedure'.[101] (Emphasis added)

According to the *Oxford English Dictionary*, 'hazardous' means 'risky;
dangerous' and that is exactly what vivisection is. All this time and money
spent on 'safety-testing' drugs and other chemicals (pesticides, herbicides,
food additives, etc.) on animals is utterly wasted. Developing numerous new
chemical compounds and trying them out for safety on animals does not give
us humans a safe-conduct to health and security. As even Professor Domer
comments on all these extensive animal tests:

> 'This has resulted in a vast amount of information being generated at a
> very large expense. The nagging problem which continues to confront
> scientists, industry and the government is that there does not appear to
> be any good evidence that this increase in [animal-experimental] work
> and expense in the development of new compounds has resulted in an
> appreciable decrease in the potential hazards for the population at large'.
> (p.71).

He is quite right. Expenditure upon vivisection constitutes an unjustified
depredation of scarce and much-needed resources.

There is one other factor which we have not yet considered and which
complicates the extrapolation picture even further: female and male animals
of the same species and same strain sometimes react very differently to the
same drug or chemical! So startling are these sex differences that they deserve
a whole chapter to themselves.

CHAPTER FIVE

Sex Differences

We have seen how different animal species respond differently to chemicals and drugs. What we must now investigate is how the different sexes of the same species can react very differently from each other. This, of course, makes the whole question of extrapolation just that bit more complicated (as if it were not already an impossible task).

Bile excretion

Many chemicals are excreted by animals in large part via their bile. Bile is a thick alkaline fluid (greenish-brown in colour) which aids digestion. It is secreted by the liver and stored in the gall-bladder, whence it is intermittently ejected into the duodenum (part of the small intestine) via the common bile duct

As the reader may well have guessed by now, animals vary in the amounts of biliary excretion which characterise them. Dr. Edward J. Calabrese of the University of Massachusetts writes: 'Numerous interspecies differences exist with respect to biliary excretion'.[102] Rats and dogs seem to be the most effective biliary excreters of a certain range of chemical compounds, whereas other animals and humans rank lower down the hierarchy in varying degrees.[103] As mentioned above, there are also *sex* divergences as regards bile excretion amongst animals. Let us look at some of these.

The chemical, tartrazine, is excreted via the bile differently as between male and female Wistar albino rats. Males excrete in 3 hours about 17% of an intravenous dose in their bile and approximately 70% in their urine, whereas females excrete as much as 40% in their bile and as little as 45% in their urine. Guinea-pigs and rabbits, on the other hand, show a less marked sex contrast in their biliary excretion of tartrazine, to the extent that male guinea-pigs excrete 33% (double the amount of male rats, however) and females 39% (almost the same as female rats), and male rabbits excrete only 5% (more than three times less than male rats) and female rabbits excrete 6% in their bile over a 3-hour period (nearly *seven times* less than female rats).

Where do healthy humans stand in all this? Nobody knows. Data are only available from *sick* human beings, and this information, as Dr. Calabrese rightly states, cannot be extrapolated to *healthy* human beings.[104] If it is not even possible to extrapolate medical data from one type of human being to another, what hope have the vivisectors of accurately transferring data relating to rabbits and rats to people?!

More sex differences in cats, rabbits and rats etc.

Another example of a sex difference is provided by the cat: male cats are twice as sensitive as females to the blood-pressure-raising effects of the hormone, noradrenaline.[105]

Even the blood pH (the measure of acidity/alkalinity) levels vary according to sex. If dihydrocodeine is injected into the veins of rabbits it causes an increase in the pCO_2 (concentration of dissolved carbon dioxide) with a decrease in the plasma bicarbonate level in male rabbits. Following administration of phenazocine to rabbits, the pCO_2 is still increased but there is little alteration in the plasma bicarbonate level in male rabbits but a marked increase in the females.[106]

Sex differences in response to a number of substances seem to occur more frequently in rats than other animals, but even within the various rat strains there will be variety, and one cannot notice any consistent trend that would indicate that the male-female response pattern will always be the same 'across the board'.[107] Reverting momentarily to bile excretion, we might note that sometimes male rats excrete more of a substance via their bile than female rats do, and sometimes females excrete more than males.[108] The data constitute a patchwork of inconsistencies and contradictions. But that is just the point: biological phenomena are not rigid and fixed (like the lauded immutable Laws of Physics). Of all the main sciences, biology is the least exact, because it is the most variable in the 'materials' with which it operates.

As touched upon earlier, rabbits can exhibit sex differences in their response to chemicals: an example of this is provided by the compound, Phenolphthalein glucuronide, 13% of which is excreted in the bile of female rabbits but only 5.1% in males.[109] Other chemicals tested on rabbits elicit a greater sex differentiation of biliary response even than is found in rats.[110]

Let us go briefly back to humans. The chemical, Epoxide hydroxylase, causes enzyme activity in the liver of humans *similar* to the *highest* values reported in pigs and rabbits, but *much higher* than those of rats and mice — the favourite laboratory animals.[111]

Sex-related differences can also be found in liver sulfatases (specific enzymes). The sulfatase C and steroid sulfatase values of young male Wistar rat livers are twice as great as those of the female liver. Mice, however, display much lower liver enzyme activities in this regard than rats, and no sex differences; yet with the DHAS synthesizing systems, a strongly marked sex difference is found, similar to that of the rat, with the female mouse displaying much greater hepatic enzyme activity than the male.[112] No sex differences in serum and urine aryl sulfatase activity have been found in humans and this seems to reflect yet another difference between rats, mice and people,[113] specifically as regards liver functioning.

Different enzyme and co-enzyme activities in the livers of other animals and humans might also be alluded to here. For example, adult male Sprague-Dawley rats show nearly twice as much glutathione S-transferase activity (with 1,2-dichloro-4-nitrobenze as a substrate) than females; yet this greater liver activity of the male rat is not uniformly seen in other studied species, where the female squirrel monkey and the female common tree shrew, for instance, exhibit more enhanced liver enzyme activity than the males, the male rhesus monkey displays greater activity than the females, but male and female pigs are almost identical in their glutathione S-transferase values. How about humans? *They display no sex-related differences in this regard.*[114]

Some vivisectors claim there is a sex difference in the susceptibility of mice to liver damage caused by carbon tetrachloride. But, as so often, other vivisectors disagree, as they have achieved conflicting results ...[115]

In 1982 the American Petroleum Institute published their findings that male rats are more liable to develop cancer of the kidneys than females when chronically exposed (for 30 hours a week for 27 months) to the fumes of uncombusted, unleaded petrol.[116] What is this supposed to tell us? That human males should not stand by a car exhaust pipe for 30 hours a week over 27 months if they don't want to damage their health? Of course women can breathe in as much petrol fumes as they like, it would seem.

The absurdity of trying to guess whether chemicals that bring about a certain reaction in one species of animal will also cause it in others (let alone humans) can be illustrated by looking at some chemicals that affect the male rat kidney and seeing if the effects are the same in other animals. The vapour of varnish and naphtha causes renal injury in male Wistar rats, but not in dogs; Stoddard solvent damages the kidneys of male Wistar rats also, but not of beagle dogs (male); JP-5 Shale jet fuel renally damages male rats but not females, and it has no effect upon dogs (male or female) or female mice. Methyl-isobutylketone causes kidney damage in male rats but not in male monkeys.[117] Are humans like monkeys or like rats in this matter? Nobody can be sure. They can only guess and hope they are right ...

Gentamicin is a widely used antibiotic. But a study in 1982 indicated a sex difference in the damage it can do to the kidneys: male rats treated with gentamicin developed severe renal dysfunction, whereas the female rats did not. And humans: are men the same as rats? *No.* Research into humans (which is the only relevant research) has found *no significant difference between the sexes.*[118]

Male mice of certain strains develop kidney damage when exposed to chloroform (a marked, coagulative type of necrosis — tissue death — occurs in the 'proximal convoluted tubules' of the kidneys), but this does not happen in female mice.[119] Can we rely upon these data for application to people? '... the extrapolative relevance of the mouse sex difference to humans remains to be established,' says Dr. Calabrese.[120] In other words he does not know if these data are relevant to humans or not. Nor will he ever know by conducting 'animal research' ...

Similarly with regard to copper: male rats are more susceptible to copper poisoning than females (who are immune to it). As for humans, Dr. Calabrese writes: 'To what extent these findings are relevant to the human situation is unknown'.[121] Yet again — as always.

Female rats are more susceptible to Hexachlorobenzene-induced porphyria (a disease condition that induces urination of porphyrins — pigments widespread in living things — inflammation/blistering of the skin and inflammation of the nerves) than male rats. Does this tell us that women should be more careful than men when coming into contact with the chemical, hexachlorobenzene, and that men are less at risk? Yes, that is precisely what the animal evidence indicates. But it is misleading. In humans, *males are at greater risk than women — the very reverse of the situation in animals.*[122]

In the case of the chemical, Cephaloridine, male rats are at greater risk of suffering kidney damage than female rats, but in mice the sex difference becomes reversed, with female mice being at greater risk of renal damage than males.[123]

The chemical, Aldrin, causes liver cancer in male mice but not in male rats; 1,2-Dibromoethane, however, causes liver tumours in the male rat but not in the male mouse. But 2-Aminoanthraquinone causes liver cancer in both of them![124] And humans?

There are innumerable such examples which we could cite to point up the utter confusion caused by looking at animals for information about people. But we fear boring the reader!

Speaking of whom, the reader may at this juncture comment: 'Surely if a chemical causes damage to the same sex of *several* species that must indicate a strong probability of the same thing obtaining in humans?' Oh, would that it were that simple! The truth is rather different, for human experience teaches that even where a chemical causes damage in a particular sex of *multiple* animal species, in most cases *no corresponding sex differences have been found to exist in human beings.*[125]

Enough said on this, I fancy. Time now to turn to a subject that chills the blood of us all: cancer.

CHAPTER SIX

Vivisection and Cancer

F or well over 100 years, the vivisectors have been torturing animals to death with artificially induced cancers in a quest to halt this scourge amongst humankind. With what results? Cancer is now occurring at the rate of 1 in 3 persons in Britain and America (people either with the illness or expected to develop it), rising soon to 1 in 2.

Cancer incidence and death rates

The survival rates of cancer sufferers have not dramatically improved. Naturopath, Patrick Rattigan, N.D., writes in his booklet on cancer: 'There has been no significant increase in survival rates since records began'.[126] In fact, between 1970 and 1991 the *death rates* from cancer of the lung, bone marrow, skin, lymph, liver, kidney, prostate, throat, and brain *increased* (*Science*, vol. 267, p.1414, 10.3.95)! So much for 150 years of 'life-saving' vivisectional research.

Even an editorial in *The Lancet* in 1996 admitted the dismal truth:

'A president of the USA 25 years ago declared a War on Cancer, confident that the war was winnable. *It has been judged, so far, LOST*. With the exception of advances in the treatment of haematological [i.e. blood] cancers, and a few others, *25 years has seen little progress*'. (Vol.348, 6.7.96, p.1; emphases added.)

Another doctor, also writing in *The Lancet*, likewise concedes that there has been '... *no decline in overall mortality*' from cancer (Dr. Michael B. Sporn in Vol. 347, 18 May 1996, p.1,378; emphasis added), while yet another doctor, oncologist Dr. Albert Braverman, states in connection with the chemotherapy approach to cancer that this treatment meets with '... almost *invariable failure*' (*The Lancet*, 13.4.91; emphases added).

Yet the media are fond of saying that cancer deaths are declining and survival is lengthening. This anomaly can easily be explained. Dr. John A. McDougall points out (as does Professor Pietro Croce in our Foreword) that any *apparent* improvement in survival rates claimed by some is in large measure the result of detecting the cancer *earlier*, so that the '5-year survival period' regarded as evidence of 'cure' (once the cancer has been zapped into temporary abeyance by chemotherapy and radiotherapy or radical surgery) in fact commences at a much earlier stage and results in an effective 'massaging' of the statistics. Dr. McDougall writes:

'The American Cancer Society ... fails to tell us that the "improved" survival rate seen over the past 80 years for most cancers is largely the result of earlier detection — not more effective treatment. Finding the cancer earlier does allow more people to live five years after the time of diagnosis. Thus more people will fit the definition of "cured". However, in most cases, early detection does not increase a person's life span but only the length of time a person is aware he or she has cancer'.[127]

The great chemist, Dr. Linus Pauling, twice winner of the Nobel Prize, is even more castigating. He does not hesitate to condemn most cancer 'research' as out-and-out fraud. A few years before his death in the early 1990s, Dr. Pauling said:

'Everyone should know that most cancer research is largely *a fraud*, and that the major cancer research organisations are derelict in their duties to the people who support them'.[128] (Emphasis added.)

Giving cancer to animals does not give a cancer cure to humans

The internationally acclaimed medical writer, Dr. Vernon Coleman, dismisses the idea that by studying cancer in animals we can learn about cancer in people. He writes:

'The real truth is that the available evidence shows that animal experiments are a waste of time, that animal experiments have never led to any useful breakthrough and that they are never likely to lead to any useful breakthroughs. The simple, unvarnished truth is that animals get different types of cancer to human beings, animals respond quite differently to drugs ... Indeed, the evidence shows that instead of helping doctors, researchers working with animals have held back medical progress and have been responsible for hundreds of thousands of deaths'.[129]

Other doctors have concurred. The eminent physician, Professor Hastings Gilford, concluded an extensive study of cancer experiments with the words:

'It has fallen to my lot to have to make a general survey of cancer in all its aspects and I do not believe that anyone who does this with an open mind can come to any other conclusion than that to search for the cause or cure of cancer by means of experiments on lower animals is useless. Time and money are spent in vain'.[130]

As recently as 1990, Professor Karol Sikora, oncologist, wrote of RNA tumour viruses which cause cancer in animals but which are of scant relevance to humans. Speaking of these viruses, Professor Sikora makes reference to this vital animal/human difference:

'These organisms, *of little relevance to human cancer*, cause a *wide range of tumours in cats, rodents, monkeys and birds*'. (*Journal of the Royal College of Physicians of London*, Vol. 24, No.3, July 1990, p.196; emphases added).

Even earlier, *The Lancet* had hinted at the essential futility of testing out chemicals on animals with artificially created cancers or even natural ones, since those cancers are *biologically different* from human ones. We read:

'Since *no animal tumour is closely related to a cancer in human beings*, an agent which is active in the laboratory may well prove useless clinically'.[131] (Emphases added.)

The reverse situation is also true: since the relevancy of animal tests is so indeterminable (prior to the human tests that are alone relevant), their indication that a substance causes cancer in animals does not mean it will also cause cancer in people. And the vivisectionists know this. In his informative book, *Betrayal of Trust*, Dr. Vernon Coleman lists dozens and dozens of drugs that were tested out on animals, found to cause health damage in those animals (including cancer), and yet were still put out onto the market — because the drug companies were well aware that the results of animal tests are *meaningless* and *irrelevant* when it comes to the human sphere.[132]

Just how meaningless animal tests for chemical carcinogenicity truly are was graphically demonstrated in the 1980s. Dr. Peter Simmons elucidates the situation:

'Tests for the potential to cause cancer usually use rats or mice. In one study, almost half of the substances causing cancer in mice didn't cause it in rats, and vice versa. If one can't apply the result of a test on a rat to a mouse, what hope is there of applying it to a human? In another study, rats and mice were exposed to 26 substances known to cause human cancer. Fewer than half caused cancer in either rats OR mice, and the author concluded that we'd be better off tossing a coin!'[133]

More recently, the deputy editor of the journal *Science* expressed a view strikingly congruent with the sentiments of Dr. Simmons above. Dr. Philip Abelson states: 'The standard carcinogen tests that use rodents are an *obsolescent* relic of the *ignorance of past decades*' (*Science*, 21 September 1990, p.1357, emphasis added). Yet another scientist dismissing a major segment of vivisectionist activity as issuing from 'ignorance'.

The fact is that frequently animals absorb and metabolise substances unpredictably differently from humans, and they eliminate them from their bodies more quickly or slowly than us. One study has found that 19 out of 23 chemicals that were tested out were *metabolised differently by rats and people*.[134] Likewise the capacity of a substance for causing cancer and other ailments will be different too in different animal species and in people.

The vivisectionists' symposium (and what it revealed)

We are now going to do something quite intriguing: we are going to eavesdrop on a conference of vivisectors, vivisectionists and pro-vivisection epidemiologists to see what they really say about the vivisection 'craft' when they know the general public is not listening in. They reveal just what enormous problems they are having making any sense of the animal data they have amassed. Of course, they did not expect a scientific anti-vivisectionist to track down the published records of their conference (published for other vivisectionist 'scientists'). So what follows represents a slight lifting of the veil that normally conceals the vivisectors' worthless work (and their own awareness of its dubiousness) from general public scrutiny.

Approaching the 1980s, a major symposium was held at a place (found to be particularly beautiful) called the Inn of the Mountain Gods (!) somewhere in America. The purpose of the conference was to take stock of what progress had been made in trying to decide what substances cause cancer in humans. To this event were invited numerous experts in the field, who gave papers of varying length and participated in the group discussions. Their comments are noteworthy.

The conference was opened by Dr. Frederick Coulston with the tone-setting words:

'A key issue today, at least in the United States, is the prediction of chemical carcinogenesis from animal data to man. We've all struggled with this problem over the years and *there is as yet no real answer*, it seems to me. *The real answer in the final analysis will be human experience* ...'[135] (Emphasis added.)

So here we have a vivisector admitting that he himself and others like him are having to struggle with a problem (transferring animal data to humans) which cannot really be resolved at all until human experience has validated or invalidated the animal-test results. By which time, of course, the animal results are irrelevant anyway.

After making this remarkable statement of position, Dr. Coulston urges his colleague experimenters to speak freely, since they will not be overheard by the press and in any case have the right to retract any of their comments later on, prior to publication of the symposium records:

'I assure you that there is no press in this room and there is no press release to be made from this meeting so you're free to say almost anything you wish with the understanding that you can delete anything you've said later, if you so desire'.[136]

It is clear that the vivisectors were anxious that their revelations about vivisection should not be broadcast across the nation into the homes of 'Joe and Jennifer Public'. That really would be letting the cat out of the bag, so to speak! Yet what we see here is from the *published* report of the conference: one can only speculate as to what was said behind closed doors, and never published.

The next rampant vivisector to address the conference is Dr. Philippe Shubik, who brings up the question of animal experiments relating to the risks of cancer from smoking:

'Clearly, we still do not have a good animal model for the most important and well-established hazard to man',

he admits.[137] This is indeed some admission, since the link between smoking and cancer is regarded by doctors (even vivisector Shubik) as probably the best documented causative link to ill-health of which modern medicine is possessed. And Dr. Shubik is here openly acknowledging that forcing smoking tests upon animals is quite plainly an inadequate method for trying to determine whether smoking causes cancer in humans. If vivisection cannot be trusted in such a huge and glaringly obvious region of pathological causation as smoking and cancer — in what can it be trusted?

Dr. Shubik also comments on coal tar, and whether that causes cancer. He admits that experiments with mice and rabbits have proven quite confusing and contradictory:

'My mentor, Dr. Berenblum, noted that there was a *considerable discrepancy* between the effects of coal tar on the mouse and on the rabbit, the rabbit being much more sensitive. This sensitivity was measured by the rapidity with which skin tumors appeared. Berenblum had become intrigued by the fact that the carcinogen benzo(a)pyrene, isolated from coal tar by Kennaway and Cook and assumed to be the active principle of coal tar, was, in point of fact, *more potent* in the *mouse* than in the *rabbit. The opposite was true of coal tar.* In fact it was found to be quite difficult to induce tumors in the rabbit with benzo(a)pyrene by injection, and induction in the skin was much, much slower than with coal tar'.[138] (Emphasis added.)

Rabbits responding one way, mice another: what a mess! Parenthetically, we might note that as recently as 1995 the experimenter, Dr. Tony Chu of Hammersmith Hospital in London, admitted that whether animal data regarding coal tar and cancer have any relevance for humans is simply unknown:

'If you paint these products [i.e. coal-tar shampoos] onto mice in the sort of concentrations that are absorbed in humans who are using the shampoos, then you can induce skin cancers. *But how that relates to the human system, nobody actually knows'.*[139] (Emphasis added.)

Progressing to 'occupational carcinogens', especially the aromatic amines, Dr. Shubik confesses that some of the most dangerous of these cancer-causing agents, such as ß-naphthylamine, '... seem to require only minute levels to induce cancer in man [but] it seems very large doses are required to induce bladder cancers in dogs and hamsters'.[140] The obvious dangers of such a discrepancy in the field of determining 'safe' exposure levels for humans need hardly be stressed. On the other hand, vivisection can generate inappropriate worry over substances which cause cancer in animals after minimal exposure, but which in humans require substantial amounts to effect analogous results:

'Here again, it seems to me, we have a discrepancy between animal data and human data. There are these extremely low levels that Dr. Maltoni has reported as producing tumors in animals, and from anything that one sees of the human data it would appear that only men exposed to very large doses have, so far, developed cancer'.[141]

In fact, Dr. Shubik goes on to say that there is a whole series of human investigations where certain characteristics of carcinogens have been established for humans, but that those characteristics '... have not been validated in animal studies or apparently are contradicted in some of them'.[142] He speaks of the animal research into the dangers of asbestos, and confesses that using animals in this area has shown itself to be utterly inadequate:

'There is absolutely no question that there is more and more asbestos around all the time ...

Clearly, right now our animal models are *totally and absolutely inadequate* to answer all the obvious questions before us'.[143] (Emphases added.)

We now know that asbestos causes cancer in humans (this from human observation, not animal tests), but for decades animal experiments proved dangerously misleading in this area as they have been with smoking and so many other medical phenomena. In the mid-1960s, the New York Academy of Sciences was able to state the following on the risks of asbestos:

'... a large literature on experimental studies has failed to furnish any definite evidence for induction of malignant tumours in animals exposed to various varieties and preparations of asbestos by inhalation or intratracheal injection'.[144]

To this day, it would seem, what constitutes 'safe' levels of asbestos exposure — based largely on animal data — continue to snatch away human life. In the mid-1990s a British school teacher contracted a disease which is known to be caused only by asbestos dust. She was assured that the levels of exposure which she had experienced were safe (safe for animals, no doubt). But a few months later — she was dead.[145] It is because vivisection is so *dangerously misleading* that many doctors (pre-eminently Professor Pietro Croce amongst them) demand its total and immediate abolition on *human-health* grounds, regardless of any question of 'animal rights' ...

※ ※

Chemical overdosing of laboratory animals

We indicated a few lines back that vivisection can engender inappropriate panic and concern over foods or chemicals which harm animals but pose no realistic threat to people. One of the reasons for this state of affairs is the vivisectors' absurd predilection for challenging the test animals with *massive doses* of a substance to evaluate its effect. We are not talking here of doses just two or three times greater than the highest likely human doses — we are speaking of doses that outpace human doses *a hundred- or even thousandfold*.[146] Such enormous amounts bear absolutely no relation to reality: they are meaningless, since almost any substance (water included) can cause health damage if excessive amounts are forced into the body.

To illustrate the absurdity of this type of testing, we shall cast our eye over a few examples. A couple of decades or so ago, the great sugar barons of America felt threatened by the marketing of a new, cheap and highly sweet rival, the synthetic 'cyclamates'. To discredit this new product, the sugar producers commissioned animal experiments to 'prove' that cyclamates were harmful to human health. The vivisectors succeeded in this, and the artificial sweetener was removed from the market. What the sugar lords did not trumpet so loudly in their press conferences was the fact that to equal the dosages of cyclamates given to the laboratory animals, a person would have to consume around *552 bottles of cyclamate-laced soft drink a day!*[147] A similar situation arose over oil of calamus, where animal tests demonstrated it to be carcinogenic: but one would have to drink something like *500 pints* of dry vermouth a day before absorbing the equivalent amounts given to the test animals.[148] Saccharin too — another artificial sweetener which threatened the profits of the giant sugar corporations — had its public image severely dented when animal tests revealed it could cause cancer: perhaps so, if we consume *800 12-ounce bottles* of saccharin-sweetened soft drink *on a daily basis!*[149] So we see that one of the commercial uses of animal experimentation is to get products *off* the market, as well as *onto* it. *Vivivsection can 'prove' virtually any substance safe or dangerous.*

The corollary of this ridiculous overdosing is that people no longer take the results seriously (quite rightly), and hence truly dangerous substances can become accepted as probably all right for humans, since no reliable safety tests have been carried out. The vivisectionist, Dr. H.F. Kraybill, speaking at our conference of researchers, tells of the dangers lurking in the vivisectors' testing method:

> 'The most toxic compounds are ... most likely to escape detection as potential carcinogens due to overdosing ... The most alarming feature in these dose selections is that the MTD [i.e. maximum tolerated dose] is, *in no way, related to potential environmental or industrial exposure in man.* In one case, the dose indicated for a life-time study in the rodent calculated to a total requirement *exceeding in pounds the annual production by a manufacturer*.[150] (Emphasis added.)

What possible credibility can such a ludicrous system of research have? In addition to the outsize doses that are routinely administered, we also have the problem of conflicting results as between different animals and different labs. Even Dr. Kraybill admits this, saying that 'too often' there is disagreement over which animal results are the 'authentic' ones:

'For example, response data from one laboratory sometimes cannot be duplicated elsewhere because of a different strain of the same species, variance in environmental conditions such as type and composition of diet, biorefractories (contaminants) in the water, pollutants in the air, animal care and/or husbandry, and others. The question then arises: *Which experimental findings and which reports are authentic and recognized as a basis for an informed decision?*'[151] (Emphasis added.)

Dr. Kraybill does not answer his own question — because he cannot. No vivisector, indeed no person on earth, can ever know which animal test result is the 'right' one until human experience has revealed the answer. Until then, vivisection leaves everybody in the dark — or worse, in the false light of a deceptive, will-o'-the-wisp security. Facing up to these little 'local difficulties' of the vivisection method, with different animals and different labs telling the vivisectors different things, Kraybill articulates a beautifully understated expression of the vivisector's utter confusion:

'These variations in response, needless to state, *perplex the investigator*. In the nonprofessional's mind, reading about these variations must conjure up some *doubts as to the authenticity of the work or the significance of the findings*.'[152] (Emphasis added.)

Kraybill is here looking into the abyss and facing TRUTH: that the work of all vivisectors is inauthentic and without significance. He even momentarily admits that the science of toxicology can *never be advanced by vivisection* as things stand today. This is the sort of statement a vivisectionist will only make to his/her colleagues, but never to the general public, who must of course remain duped if the vivisectors' careers are to be safeguarded and promoted.

Dr. Kraybill reaches the zenith of his self-flagellating expiation before his vivisectionist confrères when he dismisses the whole practice of high-dose extrapolation to humans as fundamentally invalid:

'For one to analyse, statistically, toxicity data obtained from experimental studies in animals where large doses of a chemical were given, and then predict what percent of humans may be adversely affected by a challenge at a lower dose is *not valid, biochemically or pharmacologically*.'[153] (Emphasis added.)

Well, coming from a man who has spent his entire professional lifetime associated with vivisection, this is truly a damning declaration. If the vivisectionists themselves secretly admit the invalidity of this kind of animal 'research', why should those of us who have not been brainwashed by the PR hype for vivisection have any faith in its publicly declared value? To do so would be tantamount to indulging in a conditioned form of hopeful superstition, without any basis in reason or logic.

Vivisection: all guesswork and nonsense

Dr. Kraybill is not alone in his views at this conference of vivisectionists. Dr. Frederick Coulston agrees that trying to determine the cancerogenic dangers of a substance for humans by large-dose feeding of it to animals (the usual vivisection method) is '... *just nonsense!*'[153] (emphasis added). Vivisection *is* nonsense, and increasing numbers of medical doctors and scientists are coming out and saying so. But where enormous vested interests are at stake, truth is pushed to the sidelines and not allowed a voice. The present little book is trying to fight back, to make the intelligent student of the subject *think*, and *question* what the vivisectionists (largely via the uncritical media) have been telling us so mendaciously all these years.

The fact is that the vivisectors cannot know whether a substance is going to cause human cancer or not. Dr. Coulston says so in terms:

'What he [i.e. the toxicologist-vivisector] can't tell is whether the chemical is going to cause cancer, and this is the hangup of the toxicologist today'.[154]

The reason he cannot tell is simply that animal studies bring in a mass of undigested and indigestible data which no one knows how to process for accurate application to humans. It is as though the vivisectors each had pieces of entirely different jigsaw puzzles in their hands and were attempting to make an integrated whole out of them. The pieces just will not fit and even if sometimes they do, they do so by sheer luck alone. Hardly scientific.

A distinguished toxicologist, Roy Goulding, recently confessed in the journal *New Scientist* (2.5.92) that toxicology (which of course is built upon animal tests) is not predominantly a rational practice, but a species of illogical religious worship obeyed and followed as a state-promoted faith. Goulding writes:

'Today, the subject and practice of toxicology has become exalted to the eminence and influence of a religion. It is, moreover, an established form of worship, actively supported by the State. It has its creeds and its commandments, and its hierarchy of high-priests, worshippers, adherents and novitiates. Again, like a religion, it relies rather more on faith than reason'.

These words are strikingly reminiscent of views expressed by the eminent American paediatrician, Professor Robert Mendelsohn, who in his Foreword to Hans Ruesch's *Slaughter of the Innocent* spoke of the irrational, pseudo-religious nature of modern orthodox medicine and its cult of blood sacrifices (vivisection):

> 'This wild blood-lust, starting with animal vivisection and proceeding to human mutilation, stamps Modern Medicine as the most primitive religion ever known to mankind ... I have made my choice. I have rejected as idolatrous the Religion of Modern Medicine and its fundamental sacrament — vivisection'.

Yet all the vivisection-derived data of modern medical research push to get published in 'scientific' journals. But even when, for example, the vivisectionally studied 'mechanisms' of cancer are published, some 'experts' still do not comprehend them. Dr. Ernst Wynder, a self-confessed quondam vivisector present at our vivisectionists' conference, openly admits he could not comprehend what his colleagues were publishing:

> 'For many years I've always felt as I read *Cancer Research* the articles on mechanism were so complex that *I for one, really could not understand them*'. (p.129, emphasis added).

All that animal abuse, all that 'research' — and vivisectors themselves cannot make head or tail of the data presentation when it finally comes.

Let us dwell a while longer in the region of disparate facts that the vivisectors have piled up. The experimenter, Ralph Gingell, tells the vivisection conference about the conundrum of DDT. This chemical, he says, is quite toxic to mice, inducing nervous tremors and death, with an oral LD_{50} (i.e. the amount required to prove lethal to 50% of a batch of test animals) of around 300 mg/kg. But hamsters (also rodents, the 'same' as mice) display a marked species difference, in that it takes 2,000 mg/kg of DDT to kill half of them. The vivisectors were completely baffled by this, since they could not discover any difference in the rates of absorption, metabolism and excretion that would account for the variation in response.[155] Commenting on the behaviour in animals of such chemicals (which do not seem to involve any specially reactive 'metabolites' — substances formed in, or necessary for, metabolism), vivisector Gingell admits that the results of animal tests:

> '... are very difficult, *if not impossible, to extrapolate for human safety evaluation*'.[156] (Emphasis added)

We see how when vivisectors are amongst themselves they will admit virtually anything — except, of course, that they are engaged in such pointless
research that, in all conscience, they should hand back the generous amounts
of (often public) money they are paid.

Another vivisector at this jamboree of researchers who is almost as sceptical
about extrapolation as Gingell is Dr. Ulrich Mohr from Germany. He points
out how there is a wealth of information concerning the effects of polycyclic
aromatic hydrocarbons on various tissues and organs of laboratory animals.[157]
However, he reminds his listeners that humans are exposed to these chemicals
in minute quantities over a lifetime, chemicals present in various combinations
in the forms of soot, coal tar, mineral oils, tobacco smoke, car fumes, etc.;
whereas laboratory animals are dosed up on huge quantities of isolated chemicals during a very much shorter life-span. Remarking upon such different
scenarios, Dr. Mohr confesses: 'This obviously limits the extent to which it is
feasible, or indeed expedient, to simulate human experience'[158] in the vivisection laboratory. He finally comes clean and admits:

'... to what extent the extrapolation to man of data obtained from experimental models is valid, *is a question still requiring final resolution*'.[159]
(Emphasis added.)

Statements such as these are mind-blowing. Here we have vivisectors who
have built up their careers and made their money on the basis of animal experimentation for human health research, when they do not even know whether
their 'work' has *even one iota of value or relevance*. Some of us would call this
situation of the public's having in large measure to fund this kind of nonsense
scandalous. The vivisectors' livelihoods are sustained by downright deception,
since the sad truth is that these researchers and the chemical/pharmaceutical
companies behind most of them are receiving over-generous salaries for
amassing mountains of data which on their own admission are not known to
be of any use to human beings whatsoever. As yet another experimenter, Dr.
David Clayson, confirms:

'We're accumulating a *vast number of facts*, but we are *making very little
progress* ...'[160] (Emphasis added.)

This has forever been the position of the vivisector, and it ever will be.
His/her methodology is fundamentally unsound, untenable, for it involves
searching for solutions to human health problems in the completely wrong
direction. Studying all the manifold details of pathology arising from artificially assaulted animals in sterile laboratories to learn about *human beings* is

as foolhardy as burying oneself in the signs and sounds of Chinese in order to improve one's knowledge of written and spoken English!

On the question of the accumulation of data and facts, Sir John Maddox, a famous former editor of *Nature*, has some comments which the vivisectors in their constant acquisition of ever more disparate animal data would do well to mull over and reflect upon. Sir John writes:

> 'Is there a danger, in molecular biology, that the accumulation of data will get so far ahead of its assimilation into a conceptual framework that the data will *eventually prove an encumbrance*? Part of the trouble is that excitement of the chase leaves *little time for reflection. And there are grants for producing data, but hardly any for standing back in contemplation*'. (*Nature*, 1988, 335:11. Emphasis added.)

It is interesting that Sir John (a vivisectionist) resorts to imagery of hunting and the implicit blood-lust this can stimulate. It is also telling that he is highly aware of one of the main motivating forces behind vivisection — grant money. The vivisectors are indeed piling up mountains of data, without reflection or logic, and are thus erecting an enormous 'encumbrance' on the journey to genuine knowledge. But the grants continue to roll in, and the vivisectors' bank accounts continue to prosper.

It is time for us to conclude our visit to the vivisectors' conference, but not before we lift the veil still further on the confessions to which that assembly was a witness. Perhaps, amongst other things, we should hear the final words of these experimenters as they prepare to dash back to their labs and their unending 'experiments' and get ready for another all-expenses paid 'working' holiday in beautiful parts of the world. As the vivisector, Dr. Philippe Shubik, humorously puts it towards the end of the symposium:

> 'Well, I think we've achieved *our major objective*, because I did hear Ernst say, 'If I am right', and that leaves an opening for a series of people *to do additional experiments. The chief objective here is to keep us all employed*, and to make sure we do interesting experiments *so that we can come back to these nice places*'.[161] (Emphasis added.)

'Many a true word spoken in jest' is the only comment required here.

Summing up the congress and homing in upon the central question of whether it is possible to extrapolate from animal data to human beings, Dr. David Clayson displays an amazing degree of honesty:

> '... when we come to extrapolate across the species boundaries from our experimental animals to man ... [w]hat we're doing at the moment is

politically expedient, *but don't let's pretend we're doing something scientific* …'[162] (Emphasis added.)

Dr. Clayson further hints that vivisection is pointless, because of its utter inconclusiveness and potential to mislead. He speaks of the anti-TB drug, isoniazid, and the misleading animal data on it:

'Presently, we recognize the ability of the effective antituberculosis drug, isoniazid, to induce lung adenomas [i.e. tumours] *in a wide variety of mice* which are susceptible to this tumor … In man, despite the fact that this drug has been effectively and extensively used since 1953, a period of 24 years, *I know of no convincing evidence of its carcinogenic effect in man* … Unfortunately, *we know of no sure way to differentiate accurately between those drugs and other chemicals which induce cancer in both animals and man and those which although effective in animals, are ineffective in man*' (p.193, emphasis added).

Dr. Coulston clearly shares Clayson's doubts about vivisection. He says their (the vivisectors') fallacy, is to assume:

'… that the mouse or the rat or the hamster predicts for man, and *we have no basis for this prediction* …'[163] (emphasis added).

Dr. Coulston subsequently utters a plea for help — to make sense of what he and his vivisector friends are doing:

'The real help we need is to *try to understand what we're doing … relating our animal experimentation to the human experience.* The toxicologist is limited, he's very limited, in the interpretation of animal data to man' (p.396, emphasis added).

Coulston then, astonishingly, turns on the method of vivisectionally 'safety-testing' food additives and ridicules the misplaced optimism embedded in this methodology:

'In general, we go from dogs and rats and put the additive out in the general population and *just hope for the best. It is a dreadful mistake to do this, and I've always thought this way*' (ibid., emphasis added).

Coulston of course knows that the only relevant data are those issuing from humans and not animals. He further admits that anything involving the attempt to extrapolate from animals to humans is ultimately '*a half-baked guess*'[164] (emphasis added) at a solution to the problems besetting cancer research. The vivisector, Dr. Irving J. Selikoff, likewise finds it necessary at the end of the conference to ask the key question:

'Does the animal model have any relevance to human disease? If not, *we're wasting a lot of time, a lot of money, a lot of good scientists, and a lot of space at NIH* [National Institutes of Health]'.[165] (Emphasis added.)

That such a question needs to present itself after days of vivisectional testimony is itself a damning indictment of this fatally flawed methodology.

Dr. Clayson continues the trend of honesty when he calls health policy decisions based on extrapolated animal data 'really *pseudoscientific*'[166] (emphasis added), and Dr. William M. Upholt of the U.S. Environmental Protection Agency chimes in and says:

'I completely agree with Dr. Clayson that *extrapolation is unscientific*'.[167] (Emphasis added.)

Our uncomprehending but honest vivisectionist, Dr. Ernst Wynder (he could not get to grips with the complicated articles his confrères in cancer research were writing, remember?) hits another crucial nail on the head when he confesses his own and other vivisectors' collective failure:

'I reflect that I've been in cancer research 30 years ... and during these 30 years lung cancer has continued to increase, *so we have not been very effective* ...

... what will happen to the incidence of cancer 10, 20 or 30 years from now? If the incidence does not decline, in fact, if for certain cancers it will increase, *we will certainly have not done our job effectively*' (pp.392 and 226, emphasis added).

No, the vivisectionists have not done the job publicly entrusted to them — to liberate humanity from disease. Twenty years after Dr. Wynder spoke the above words, the cancer incidence and death rates continue to rise...

Perhaps the best, clearest summary statement of the ever-speculative nature of vivisection comes from Dr. Frederick Coulston, who confesses that using animals to gain biological knowledge about human reactions to chemicals is guesswork from beginning to end. Yet he and his colleagues display such a paucity of imaginative powers that they cannot think beyond the narrow horizons of vivisectional practice. Dr. Coulston affirms:

'It's tough enough to prove efficacy [i.e. of chemicals and drugs], let alone proving safety. What I'm trying to say is, that we should resolve the problem by asking ourselves, 'Is the rodent or the hamster predicting something to man?' and then spend our time trying to find that out ...

[Again, he does not know whether all the myriads of animal tests are predicting anything relevant at all.]

Let's do the metabolism studies which tell us whether these animals are truly handling the chemical like man. We've heard no discussion of that in this meeting, by the way. But that's what happens when toxicologists get together. I'm simply trying to say that *this is **ALL GUESS***, and as David Clayson said *we shouldn't put too much faith in it*; yet I don't know how to do it better'.[168] (Emphases added.)

To which the vivisector, Dr. Irving Selikoff (like Coulston, aware of vivisection's inadequacy but unable to think of anything more scientific or sensible), replies with unabashed alacrity: '*I think we have to agree with you*' (p.392, emphasis added).

Yes. The vivisectors have here truly revealed their hand. They know vivisection is '*all guess*', but are unable or unwilling to break free from the rut of tradition-bound, establishment thinking (or the perks that go with it). So animal experimentation continues as a cruel guessing game (in which we should place *no* faith whatever), paid for at enormous expenditure in time, money and sacrificed animal and human lives.

Before we leave the topic of cancer altogether, we must just look at the major bugbear of cancer research — the phenomenon known at 'metastasis', that is, the spread of cancer from its original site to different parts of the body. Let's briefly take a fresh chapter for this topic.

CHAPTER SEVEN

Cancer Metastasis

M ost cancer patients who fail to survive the disease do not die of the primary (initial) tumour, but of cancer 'metastasis' — the spread of cancer from its first site to other areas of the body. These metastases have been the subject of research for decades, with experimenters trying to replicate and extrapolate from them in animal models. They have failed signally.

Firstly, artificially carcinogen-challenged laboratory animals do not normally develop metastases at all (this is recognised almost as a hallowed Law amongst vivisectors), and in any case the cells which make up the animal tumour are different from those characterising human cancers. Even within a single *human* patient the cancer cells will be heterogeneous (diverse in character). Cells from the same tumour can display different surface properties, different antigenicity (antigens are substances that the body regards as foreign and makes antibodies against), different immunogenicity, different growth rates, different karyotypes (sets of chromosomes), different sensitivity to various cell-destroying drugs, and different potential for metastasising (proliferating further) into other areas of the body.[169] So if cancer cells differ within the same person, let alone between different people, what sense does it make to study cancer cells in animals, which are even further removed from the individual human patient?

Vivisectors yet again question vivisection's validity

Writing in the mid-1980s, the vivisectors, Dr. J. Fidler and Dr. Raffaella Giavazzi, refer to the current animal models for cancer as having 'little clinical relevance'.[170] The two researchers also confess that using animals for cancer-data extrapolation to humans is of dubious soundness:

> 'Whether experimental tumor systems are valid models for therapeutic modalities for human cancer, or indeed whether specific therapeutic modalities shown to be effective in one animal tumor system can be applied to another system, is debatable'.[171]

In 1986 the records of another congress of cancer vivisectors were published, and as with the previous conference (see foregoing chapter) a good deal of interesting revelations as to the fundamental inappropriateness of animal models are made manifest. One vivisector tells of how they have been trying, without success, to find a drug against metastases, and how they have tested out (on animals) some *one million* substances in just *25 years*. As that vivisector, Dr. Kurt Hellmann, an employee of Britain's Imperial Cancer Research Fund, rightly comments:

> 'The take home message is: that if we have not found a selective anti-cancer drug amongst the first million substances screened, will it be any more likely amongst the second million'.[172]

Clearly not. But the 'take-home message' for us is that the last thing these cancer researchers need is a genuine *cure* for cancer, since they (and their extremely wealthy funding 'cancer charities') would be out of a job. So the search goes on in the obviously wrong direction. We might add at this point that cancer has been successfully treated for many, many years by *holistic, natural* means (predominantly through a vegan diet and positive mental strategies) — but there is not a lot of profit to be made by the giant pharmaceutical industry from encouraging people to give up meat, and to eat large quantities of organically grown chickpeas, apricot and apple seeds, for example, plus lots of Vitamin C and Vitamin B17, and to practise meditation and relaxation, as well as maintain an optimistic and positive mental attitude![173]

Another experimenter reports how a large number of clinical (that is, human) trials of immunotherapeutic strategies against cancer proved substantially unsuccessful. The mistake, of course, was to base these trials on the results of 'animal model' experiments:

> 'In retrospect, it is obvious that many of the clinical trials were based on assumed extrapolation from *promising animal models*, even though it was clear that *extrapolation from one animal model to another, let alone from animal model to human disease, was frequently not possible*'.[174] (Emphasis added.)

Correction: extrapolation is *never* possible. If we may divert slightly for a moment, we might consider the LD_{50} test, where members of the the same species of animal (usually rodents), of the same age and strain, in the same laboratory are fed the same test-substance until 50% of them die — some die quickly, some slowly, some only sicken, others survive relatively unscathed after being force-fed that same chemical: so if even within the exact same species in the exact same laboratory experimenters cannot reliably predict reactions from one animal to its neighbour, what hope in heaven have they got of predicting from animals to humankind?

Even humans themselves vary across and within the ethnic groups. It is now well known, for example, that most Oriental adults are intolerant to the milk sugar, lactose, because of the low level of lactase in their small intestine, whereas most northern Europeans are able to absorb lactose without any trouble (*Ethnic Differences in Reactions to Drugs and Xenobiotics*, ed. Kalow, Goedde and Agarwal, Alan R. Liss, 1986, p.29). Automatically to assume that drugs will have the same effect on whites, blacks and orientals is almost as medically inept and myopic as extrapolating from animals to humans. As Dr. Price Evans rightly states: '... it is not permissible to make blind extrapolations regarding the effects of drug therapy from one drug to another *or from one ethnic group to another*' (ibid, p.503, emphasis added).

But let us return to our cancer vivisectors and what they secretly admit when no members of the press are present to report their words to the public. In cancer research the investigators often inject mouse or human tumour cells into mice to study cancer in humans. It sounds foolish, and it is foolish. Firstly, mice will respond to an influx of cancerous cells into their body in ways different from humans (the immune system is different), and equally, the very method of creating cancer in these animals is artificial. Humans do not get cancer by someone injecting it into them! Except, of course, through vaccination (where, for instance, the Salk polio-virus vaccine was contaminated with the potentially carcinogenic SV-40 monkey virus). But vaccination is so vast a field of medical damage ('iatrogenic illness' — illness caused by doctors) that we cannot devote space to it in this little volume.[175] Anyhow, the artificial (and therewith misleading) nature of this mode of generating cancer in animals through injection is correctly criticised by the vivisectors themselves:

'A few people like Josh Fidler and Jorgen Fugh have been saying that its (sic!) *biologically incorrect* to inoculate epithelial mouse or human tumors into mice subcutaneously and *expect them to behave like humans*. In other words, you are *not recapitulating the natural history of the carcinoma*' [i.e. cancer].[176] (Emphasis added.)

Thus states Dr. D. R. Welch. But it does not stop there, as Dr. Welch (himself a vivisector) owns up, for melanomas (usually, skin cancers) rarely show evidence of spread in 'nude' mice (that is, hairless, thymus-deprived mice) to the major organs (e.g. liver, brain, and especially to other parts of the skin) to which human melanoma usually extends. Dr. Welch says he knows of no report in the world's vivisection literature where skin metastases (skin cancer spread) have been observed with the B16 melanoma, K1735 melanoma or indeed any human melanoma grown in nude mice.[177] Even when the vivisector is introducing *human* cells into the animals, the methodology is still fundamentally flawed since, as Dr. Welch clearly indicates:

'... if the growth and malignant behavior of that tumor in a nude mouse doesn't recapitulate its natural history in man, then the *validity of that model is questionable even though it is human in origin and therefore is "more relevant"* '.[178] (Emphasis added.)

The same, incidentally, might be said of 'gene transfer' experiments, which put one or two human genes into animal 'models' to study human illness — the whole process is still so artificial, unpredictable and, overall, so unlike the human biological/psychological/social situation that it is ultimately meaningless and pointless.

Most of us will know someone with cancer, and most of us will have been saddened by their loss. We even think of such popular entertainers as Roy Castle and Marti Caine, who, after a highly publicised struggle and the best orthodox treatment money could buy, failed to be cured of this dreadful disease. Yet the cancer doctors and researchers will, in public at least, constantly be assuring us that they are making major strides forward and that a cure for cancer is 'just around the corner'. What such researchers (read 'vivisectors') say amongst themselves is rather different.

Dr. John N. Weinstein and his colleagues — all specialists in cancer 'research' — do not hesitate to reveal their pessimism regarding the conquest of cancer when they appear at a get-together with their vivisectionist compeers. Experience has taught them that the tried orthodox methods are simply not working and not likely to work in any substantial way:

'To emphasize again what has been said many times, our attempts to deal with established cancers are generally *doomed*, not by the primary tumor, but by *our inability to detect and eradicate metastases*'.[179] (Emphasis added.)

In recent years a new approach has been tried using 'monoclonal antibodies'. These are antibodies produced artificially from a cell clone and consisting of a single type of immunoglobulin. But even here success has been strikingly limited:

'Despite the opportunity provided by this tumor cell selectivity, the clinical results with monoclonal antibodies to date have been *modest at best*'.[180] (Emphasis added.)

This, of course, was despite the promise held out by the preceding animal studies. But the simple fact is that all of these animal models of cancer do not adequately relate to the human situation, to treatments that will work in human patients. Dr. James E. Talmadge makes this quite plain when he speaks of animal research into cancer that involves ascites (swelling of the abdomen, because of the accumulation of fluid in the peritoneal cavity):

'One thing we can say is that the preclinical 'in vivo' [i.e. animal] ascites models *do not correlate well with clinical* [i.e. human] *therapeutic activity*. I think that's one thing we can set aside and go on ...'[181] (Emphasis added.)

Yes. Such animal models should indeed be set aside, as they are worse than useless.

What may well come as a shock to the reader who has hitherto perhaps had an almost religious faith in medical 'research' is that the researchers themselves all too frequently do not really understand what they are saying or know what they are doing. Extreme? Overstated? Not at all. We have already heard from Drs. Wynder and Coulston on this in the previous chapter. Now let us listen to what another experimenter, Dr. Talmadge, admits. He tells of how researchers do not know how to establish whether their manipulations of animal models can be reliably linked to the human cancer patient at all:

'We are not even sure which experiments we can do to prove there is a correlation between preclinical [i.e. animal] and clinical [i.e. human] models',

says Dr. Talmadge.[182] Again, what is so breathtaking about this type of statement is that it shows the vivisectors have been using for over 150 years a method of which they have absolutely no knowledge that it has any relevance to human health whatsoever. It is a case of blind, unintelligent following of tradition without the courage to question and oppose — and radically to change course. There is no genuinely 'scientific' approach operating here, only obedience to the authority of tradition. One vivisector calls their attitude to animal experimentation 'naive' — 'We are still somewhat naive' says Dr. Garth L. Nicolson[183] — but we could think of other adjectives to apply to such laboratory jokers ...

Orthodox cancer treatments: doing more harm than good?

The tragedy, of course, is that the vivisectors' bungling had led, and is at this very minute still leading, to human disaster and death. We have ended up with a situation where the orthodox cancer 'treatment' can do far more harm than good. The vivisectors are fully aware of this ('naiveté' simply does not come into it). Here is what some of these laboratory workers confess:

'Actually, I think that the drugs that we have are not doing very many people much good'. — Dr. McGovren.[184]

'Unfortunately, all too frequently, conventional therapy can indirectly lead to patient morbidity [i.e. disease] and mortality [i.e. death] through immune compromise [i.e. damage to the immune system] and the resulting infectious complications'. — Dr. Lance A. Liotta.[185]

'It now seems apparent that we can add to this list [i.e. of problems faced by the cancer patient] another problem that until only very recently has been largely ignored or unappreciated, namely, that almost any form of [orthodox] cancer therapy has the potential to exacerabate [sic!] or amplify the malignant capacity of tumor cells. This can occur for a variety of reasons, e.g. induction of localized damagae [sic!] to host tissues such as endothelial cells that line blood vessels, thereby facilitating attachment or adhesion of tumor cells; or it can be related to the induction of genetic and/or epigenetic changes in the genome of tumor cells, *thereby leading to the emergence of new and more aggressively behaving mutant tumor cell phenotypes*'. — Dr. R.S. Keibel et al.[186] (Emphasis added.)

'Immunosuppression caused by *therapy* which results in infections *is what kills the patient*, not really the metastatic burden'. — Dr. Liotta again.[187] (Emphasis added.)

and:

'... there are well documented cases where chemotherapeutic treatment of a patient actually worsened the disease process. These patients *died much sooner than would have been expected* and with *more widespread disease than was present before the treatment*'. — Dr. Nicolson.[188] (Emphasis added.)

The 'treatment' killing off patients quicker than the cancer itself: this is a scandal. Yet the public continue to accept it, as they are constantly being lied to by those with vested interests in the cancer business (I use the word advisedly) into a tragically misplaced belief that the 'researchers' are making great leaps forward. No wonder iatrogenic (doctor-induced) disease is probably at an all-time high this century: Dr. Patrick Pietroni, Senior Lecturer in General Practice at St. Mary's Hospital Medical School, claimed in 1990 that at any given time something like one out of every six hospital patients has been put in that situation because of the serious 'side-effects' of drugs administered by doctors. Dr. Vernon Coleman suspects that the figure is even higher.[189] Needless to say, *all* of those harmful drugs were passed as 'safe' after extensive tests on animals.

Here we arrive at a most important proof of vivisection's failure: the number of drug disasters that have blighted trusting patients' lives. Whole books have been written (e.g. by Hans Ruesch, and by Vernon Coleman) on this subject. But in the present study we have space for only a brief chapter devoted to drug damage.

CHAPTER EIGHT

Drug Damage

'There is no such thing as a safe drug,'[190] declared Dr. Hamish Cameron, head of medical affairs for the drug manufacturer, Zeneca, in 1995. And this after decades of using animals to try to make drugs safe. As we saw in the last chapter, animal-tested drugs can do more damage than the illnesses they are supposedly designed to cure.

Animal tests are clearly useless. Indeed, most pharmaceutical research (which routinely uses animals in the thousands) has been characterised by the medical expert, Dr. H. Stähelin, as being typified by '... *usual, frequent failures* and ... *rare* success' (emphasis added) ('Cyclosporin: Historical Background', in *Prog. allergy*, 38, 1985, pp. 19-27).

There are numerous drugs which were put onto the market in recent decades after thorough animal safety-tests but which had to be withdrawn subsequently, since they caused unforeseen damage to human patients. Dr. Vernon Coleman has listed around 83 drugs withdrawn from European markets between 1961 and 1993.[191] What is remarkable is that the health authorities cannot even agree which drugs are sufficiently dangerous to be withdrawn, for the same drug that is banned in one country will be allowed in another. Different vivisectors obtaining different results? A number of drugs were withdrawn because of out-and-out fraudulent 'research' or suppressed data (such as apparently in the case of Debendox).[192] Other drugs proved harmful because of the way they reacted with other drugs taken by the patient. Even the vivisectionists admit that their 'animal models' are simply not relevant in areas such as this, or in the important area of allergic responses of human patients or the interaction of different diets with particular drugs. All these, and more, factors of high importance are dismissed by the professional defenders of vivisection as being 'not relevant to experimental investigation of toxicity'.[193] How paltry and pathetic are the claims made by the vivisectors for their method of safety-testing, when they do not even take into consideration something which every last normal man, woman and child on this planet must do — namely, eat and drink! Many other drugs are just downright poisonous in ways not predicted by animal studies — even the paid defenders of vivisection, the Research Defence Society (RDS) of London, admit that some 37 drugs were withdrawn in just over three decades due to toxicity *not predicted by animal experiments*.[194] And what we must remember here is that the evidence against a drug must be extremely strong for that drug to be withdrawn from circulation, since in such a scenario everyone involved, from the vivisectors and the pharmaceutical company responsible, to the Government and the prescribing doctors, ends up with egg on their face. There are countless drugs out there which are daily doing harm but which have not yet been pulled in. Remember: '*There is no such thing as a safe drug*' ...

Let us look at just a few of the numerous drugs that have caused human health disasters, despite their being 'safety'-tested on animals. I stress that the following is just a very small sample of dangerous drugs.

Thalidomide is the most notorious of damaging 'medicines', since this sedative, given to pregnant women in the 1950s and 1960s for morning sickness, caused terrible birth defects in their babies. This was not predicted by the preceding animal studies, nor was it convincingly demonstrated by subsequent tests upon all manner of pregnant animals. Dr. H. Werner Goedde, an expert on human genetics, speaks of the hazards inherent in attempts at extrapolating from animals to humans and cites Thalidomide as a prime example of this:

> '... it is often dangerous to assume that data from other species are applicable to human beings. Mostly, it is unlikely that lower animals could be used to predict mutagenesis, carcinogenesis and teratogenesis in man; an important example is the teratogenic effects of thalidomide'. (From: *Ethnic Differences in Reactions to Drugs and Xenobiotics*, ed. by Werner Kalow, H. Werner Goedde and Dharam P. Agarwal; Alan R. Liss 1986, p.16.)

The supreme anti-vivisectionist author, Hans Ruesch, admirably sums up the situation regarding Thalidomide testing after the tragedy had struck:

> '... doses of Thalidomide ... were force-fed to various strains of dogs, cats, mice, rats, and as many as 150 different strains and substrains of rabbits, with negative results. Only when the white New Zealand rabbit was tested, a few malformed rabbit babies were obtained, and subsequently also some malformed monkeys — after years of tests, hundreds of different strains and millions of animals used. But researchers

immediately pointed out that malformations, like cancer, could be obtained by administration of practically any substance in high concentration, including sugar and salt ...'[195]

In fact, New Zealand white rabbits had to be given doses of Thalidomide that were *300 times greater than the human dosage* to generate birth deformities in their offspring (Keller and Smith, in *Teratogenesis, Carcinogenesis, and Mutagenesis*, 1982, Vol. 2, pp. 361-374).

Such massive doses as were given to those test animals had no bearing on normal human consumption of the Thalidomide drug. To this day, the experimenters have not published the results of any tests that might have been done using human-equivalent doses in the animals (not that this would prove anything, anyway). With sickening hypocrisy, the arch-defenders of vivisection, the Research Defence Society, try to explain this fact away by saying that '... no definitive dose-response studies have been carried out — *these would be time-consuming and wasteful of animal life.*'[196] (Emphasis added.) How low can you sink in trying to defend an untruth? For the vivisectors to feign concern for animal life really is the ultimate in shamelessness and hypocrisy. The real reason that those (in any case irrelevant) tests have never been publicly written about is because they obviously do not indicate the massive damage which human beings would suffer at the hands of the vivisectors' wonder-drug, Thalidomide.

There are so many drugs which we could mention in connection with human health damage. The anti-diarrhoea drug, Clioquinol, for instance, caused blindness and/or paralysis three decades ago in at least 30,000 people and thousands of others died. Isoprenaline, used in aerosol inhalers for asthmatics, killed at least 3,500 children and youngsters in the 1960s — the foolish vivisectors not even realising until too late that an asthmatic fighting for breath might respond differently to a chemical spray from the manner in which a non-asthmatic dog will react. In the 1970s ICI's heart drug, Eraldin, caused 23 deaths and hundreds of victims of eye, skin and stomach damage. In the early 1980s the arthritis drug, Opren, caused 61 deaths and serious injury to 3,000 people. In the late 1980s the heart drugs, Encainide and Flecainide, caused an estimated 3,000 deaths. In 1992 Boots' heart drug, Manoplax, caused so many deaths (still unspecified) that it had to be withdrawn in under a year, despite its having received the prior attention of presumably some of Britain's best vivisectors, who tested it out on animals for nearly a decade. In 1993 the anti-shingles drug, Sorivudine, killed 14 people when combined with an 'anti-cancer' drug. In 1994 corticosteroids for asthma patients caused at least one child's death and other steroids harmed thousands of other patients. In 1994 the antibiotic, Septrin, was implicated in the causation of serious side-effects such as genital blistering, vision damage and epilepsy. The manufacturer, Wellcome, even admitted that there had been human deaths too — '... just over 100 possible fatal adverse reactions'[197] to their product — and in 1995 the Government urged restriction,[198] but the drug is still on the market...

Most of us have heard of the tragic plight of ex-Superman actor, Christopher Reeve, who fell off his horse and damaged his spine, losing the ability to walk. In 1995 the doctors at the Kessler Rehabilitation Institute, where Christopher Reeve was undergoing therapy, gave him an 'experimental' drug, 'Cygen' (first safety-tested on animals, of course) which had the highly therapeutic effect of — *stopping the actor's heart*. There followed a desperate race against time as the specialists, fearing brain damage and worse, tried to restore Reeve to life. Fortunately, they managed to get the actor's heart going again just in time — but it was a close call.[199]

The suffering and distress caused by one animal-tested product, Canesten 10% VC (vaginal cream to treat 'thrush'), was so intense that in the 1990s it drove one patient to suicide, to avoid the unbearable pain it had triggered off.[200] And in the mid-1990s also two teenagers died and 20 others suffered serious health problems, including severe arthritis and hepatitis, leading to a liver transplant, because of an antibiotic, 'minocycline', prescribed to treat common acne! (*The Sun*, 19.1.96.)

In 1987, 125 medical preparations containing barbiturates for the relief of pain were withdrawn from the German market, since they had a high risk of causing addiction (difficult to note in a rat!) and diminished physical reactions to stimuli.[201]

In 1987, 62 preparations containing metamizol (a pain-killer) were likewise withdrawn as, in addition to killing the pain, they also killed some of the patients...

In Britain alone today there are *half a million* people whose hearing has been damaged by animal-tested drugs, including antibiotics (leaflet issued by the Hearing Research Trust entitled, *Can You Help Us Defeat Deafness*, 1996).

In 1996 a drug designed to save diabetics from kidney disease and nerve damage was withdrawn following the *deaths* of two patients. The drug, Alredase — taken by an estimated 20,000 insulin-dependent diabetics — also caused one in 20 users to suffer sometimes *irreversible liver damage* (*Daily Mail*, 21.10.96).

What doctors think of the drug companies: human clinical trials

It would be easy to fill the whole of this book with examples of serious drug damage inflicted upon patients by a pharmaceutical industry that according to a MILPRO report is believed by 71% of doctors polled to be '*profit* oriented' and is associated with 'honesty' by a mere *12%* of polled doctors (*UK Prix Galien* 1995, p.22) and which carries out far more animal tests of its products (approximately 100 thousand animals are used for the testing of each drug according to German doctor, Dietrich Bässler, of the organisation 'Ärzte Gegen Tierversuche') than sensible trials upon human volunteers. These human clinical trials on average involve around only 1,480 persons according to Dr. Vernon Coleman in *Betrayal of Trust*, or around 1-3,000 in number according to the vivisectionists. Early-stage ('Phase I') human trials can involve as few as 20-80 people, and even the Phase II trials on patients with the targeted disease can number only approximately 100 volunteers, and the Phase III trials only around 1,000 persons (see the Prospectus of August 1996 for the Neotherapeutics drug company, p.27). Professor Michael Rawlins, Chairman of the Committee on Safety of Medicines, recently stated that '... on average, only 1,500 patients will have been exposed to a new product at the time of licensing' (*The Guardian*, 25.11.96). This is a fraction of the numbers who will be exposed to the drug once it is let loose by doctors upon the unsuspecting public.

Equally disturbing is that drug trials are generally carried out on *men* (*British Medical Journal*, 9.11.96) despite the fact that it is *women* who visit the doctor more frequently and can, and do, sometimes respond differently to drugs from men (but not, of course, reliably like female *animals!*).

Anyone who wishes to read further of the damage to human health caused by vivisection-processed drugs and procedures could do no better than to read *Naked Empress or the Great Medical Fraud* by Hans Ruesch. Fortunately, a few brave doctors are beginning to question just how safe and effective 'allopathic' (drug) medicine really is. One such physician is Dr. William G. Pickering, MRCP. Writing recently in *The Lancet*, Dr. Pickering expresses unease over a) the fact that many treatments are given without need or benefits to the patient; b) that treatments can be dictated by medical fashion rather than medical requirement; c) that there is absolutely no encouragement for a doctor to report useless treatments to the authorities, and d) that many drugs have harmful 'side-effects'. Dr. Pickering states quite bluntly that '... it is highly likely that a large proportion of treatments, not to say investigations and referrals, are *no more than a face-saving disguise for medical impotence.*' (*The Lancet*, February 10, 1996, p.379, emphasis added). He further insists that evidence abounds which shows the uselessness and *dangers* of many medical treatments, where their results '... create a problem infinitely worse than the original' (ibid.) and where doctors '... pile in uncritically' (ibid.) and '... deliver the *fashionable* choice in medical intervention as if *by rote*' (ibid. emphasis added). Dr. Pickering fears that consistent *quality* in medical practice will '... remain a dream' (ibid.) if doctors do not take full responsibility for what they are doing, and carry on doling out therapeutic tokens '... many of which are *overly dangerous* ...' (ibid., emphases added). Dr. Pickering concludes by saying that if the existing situation is not improved, we shall continue to see operations being performed because 'they are the fashion'; unnecessary and sometimes *harmful* investigations such as repeated radiography being carried out, and the drugs bill steadily rising (it grew by 14% in 1993) — '... although *side-effects will continue to be the only effect of many*' (ibid., emphasis added). How right Hans Ruesch, Professor Robert Mendelsohn, Dr. Vernon Coleman, Patrick Rattigan and many others have been to warn the public of the hazards of vivisectionally derived medications.

With all the above-quoted disaster stories still ringing in our ears, it is difficult to credit the audacity of the vivisectors when they claim that virtually every major advance in medicine has come about through animal experimentation. Yet that is what they claim (in public). Let us look, fairly briefly, at some of the facts.

CHAPTER NINE

A Whistle-Stop Tour Through Some Salient Points of Medical History

T he supporters of vivisection are very fond of telling the public that all major medical progress owes a great debt to animal experimentation. We do not have space to go into every reckless claim such people make, but can only look at a few of the main and frequent assertions that issue from their lips and pens (or word-processors).

Of course the main point that the open-minded student must hold on to is the fundamental principle that no animal experiment with a new chemical or technique can ever give a guarantee or even a strong probability of the same results being obtained in a human as were obtained in the animal test. Therefore, *all animal experiments are an indulgence in time-wasting speculation at best and fatally misleading guesswork at worst.*

Hardly a ringing endorsement for a practice that likes to consider itself 'scientific'.

The circulation of the blood

To begin our little foray into medical history, we could do no better than explode the old chestnut that the circulation of the blood was discovered through vivisection. Here are the facts.

An understanding of the importance of the blood is found as far back as some 3,000 or so years ago, when Moses said that the blood was the life of the body. Some 400 years before Christ, Plato wrote in his *Timaeus* of the body's being irrigated like a garden by channels of blood; and the existence of valves in the veins was observed and pointed out by Fabricius of Aquapendente (Harvey's teacher) in the sixteenth century.[202]

Dr. Moneim A. Fadali, thoracic surgeon, gives even more fascinating indications of just how old humankind's understanding of the blood, the heart and the circulation truly is. He writes:

'We did not discover through vivisection the inner chambers of the heart and the flow of warm blood in our veins and arteries. The Ebers Papyrus (1550 BC) includes a surprisingly accurate description of the circulatory system, depicting the existence of blood vessels through the entire body and the heart functioning as the center of the blood supply. In 1240 AD Ibn Al Nafis discovered the pulmonary circulation. He was director of the Nasiri Hospital in Cairo, and his dissections were performed on cadavers obtained from cemeteries in Cairo and Damascus. He proved that the blood circulates from the right side of the heart to the lungs, where it is aerated before reaching the left side of the heart. Thus, Galen's theory that blood flows from the right side of the body to the left through an opening in the intervening septum was finally laid to rest. Galen, the second century AD physician, is considered the founder of experimental physiology. His erroneous conclusions, which misled the Western world for 11 centuries, were based on animal research'.[203]

Now we come to the famous William Harvey, who 'discovered' the circulation of the blood in the West. It is true that he did perform vivisections, but it is not true that his understanding of the blood circulation derived from them. Let us hear what the great Dr. Walter Hadwen has to say on this subject:

'[Harvey's] famous book *De Motu Cordis*, in which he demonstrated the circulation of the blood, was published in 1628 ...

Harvey and his compeers knew of arteries and veins because they could see them. Harvey, from the fact that veins possessed valves, drew the conclusion that the blood which entered them was bound to flow on and could not flow back; consequently the blood reached these veins *somehow* from the arteries, but he did not know how ... and when in 1661 (that is, thirty-three years after Harvey published his famous work) Malpighi, by means of the microscope (which he had invented forty years before) discovered the capillary system of blood vessels, the mystery of the connecting link between arteries and veins was solved, which, for the lack of knowing had left Harvey's demonstration incomplete. I daresay Harvey was still further assisted in his conclusion by the fact that Berengar, more than a century before, had noted as the result of anatomical research that the aortic valve of the heart only opened *from* the heart and refused to allow the blood to return. So it was bound to go on through the arteries somewhere or other. ... the circulation could be fully demonstrated in a dead body ... and Harvey did that very thing. It is recorded in the *Life and Works of William Harvey* that he experimented on the body of a man who had been hanged by tying, in turn, the arteries and veins leading into and out of the chambers of the heart and forcibly injecting water into the heart. In fact, it may be seen any day in the dissecting room of a medical school, where a solution of red lead is forced into the left side of the heart in order to preserve the body and to show up all the vessels so that the student might easily dissect them out; and it finds its way everywhere throughout the whole body; thus demonstrating the truth of the circulation of the blood in the same simple manner that Harvey demonstrated it three centuries before'.[204]

Harvey also did simple ligaturing experiments with his own arm, as Dr. Fadali explains:

'... the historical record shows clearly that it was Harvey's careful reasoning from simple experiments with his own arm and with cadavers that led him to the theory that the blood circulates. This theory contradicted the Galenic notion that the blood ebbs and flows like the ocean's tide. By tying a ligature around his arm and noticing that the blood only accumulated on one side, Harvey deduced that the blood must move in a circuit. Despite a lifetime of animal experimentation, Galen failed to figure out that the blood circulates'.[205]

We might add that the reason Harvey did not admit the real method of his great discovery until the end of his life was that performing dissections on dead human subjects was *forbidden* in the England of those days. If Harvey had written down the true manner of his investigation, i.e. using human corpses, he would have been in great personal danger of penal retribution from the state or even an outraged public. Thus he kept his secret until shortly before his death, when he revealed it to his biographer, the Honourable Robert Boyle.

Anaesthetics and surgery

One of the chief causes of surgery's advances was the discovery of anaesthetics. The basic anaesthetics owed nothing to vivisection. Let Dr. Hadwen speak again:

'... Sir Lauder Brunton admitted to the Royal Commission on Vivisection in regard to chloroform (Q.7118-9) that 'The definite experiments in regard to its anaesthetic action were really made by Professor

Simpson on himself and on Dr. Matthews Duncan and one or two others.' That was in 1847. Then take nitrous oxide gas —which was the earliest of the anaesthetics; this was used by Mr. Jas. Stoddart and Mr. (afterwards Sir Humphry) Davey on themselves in 1801. As to aether, which is, perhaps, used more frequently than any other anaesthetic, it was tried for the first time by Dr. Morton (pupil of Horace Wells, dentist, of Hartford, Connecticut) instead of nitrous oxide, on dental patients in 1846, and was first used in England in December of the same year by Liston on human patients. Animals had nothing to do with the discovery of any of them. In fact, I am credibly informed that, had animal experiments been relied upon in any of these cases, we should have been so misled that probably humanity would have been robbed of this great blessing of anaesthesia — one of the greatest blessings, I suppose, ever conferred upon mankind'.[206]

Just how correct Dr. Hadwen is we can learn from some relatively recent experiences with a modern anaesthetic called 'fluroxene'. This anaesthetic is so deadly to laboratory animals that, if those animal tests had been heeded, it would not have been released for valuable use in hospitals. But let an avid vivisector, M. J. Halsey, relate the story:

'One of the most dramatic examples of *misleading evidence from animal data* is provided by the studies on fluroxene. After more than a decade of apparently safe clinical use, the agent was demonstrated to be *lethal* if given in long or repeat exposures in the dog, cat and rabbit, mice and rats. *If these particular experiments had been carried out 20 years earlier, the agent would never have been released*'.[207] (Emphasis added.)

So vivisection can deprive us of valuable medical tools, as well as afflict us with deadly ones, since it is so untrustworthy in its methodology and results. Further on the matter of anaesthesia, another animal experimenter, Professor Paul Flecknell, reveals the variations in response between different species when he writes in a 1993 issue of the *British Journal of Anaesthesia* on the anaesthetic, propofol, which is effective in rats, mice, dogs, cats, pigs and sheep, but *causes severe respiratory depression in rabbits*. This, of course, can lead to death. Experimenter Flecknell is also compelled to confess:

'Other commonly used human anaesthetic regimens are ineffective in some animal species, for example midazolam and other benzodiazepines do not produce unconsciousness in dogs and cats, and may cause agitation and excitement when administered by i.v. injection'. (*BJA*, 71, 1993, pp.885-894.)

Briefly on the more general question of surgery, we do not hesitate to state that surgeons learn their skills by progressively advanced experience upon cadavers and living human beings (under the watchful eye of their teacher, initially), and not by practising upon the anatomically different, and differently textured, bodies of animals. In fact, the use of animals for the development of manual dexterity in surgery is generally prohibited in the United Kingdom (yet we still produce world-class surgeons). One of the greatest British surgeons who ever lived, Lawson Tait, originally believed in vivisection but turned against it after lengthy experience showed him how misleading it was. Tait, perhaps the greatest abdominal surgeon of the 19th century and one of the founders of life-saving *aseptic* (rather than the death-dealing Listerian carbolic antiseptic) surgery, wrote of vivisection:

'I urge against it … that it has proved useless and misleading, and that in the interests of true science its employment should be stopped so that the energy and skill of scientific investigations should be directed into better and safer channels'.[208]

So strongly, in fact, did Lawson Tait believe that vivisection was the wrong path for medicine in general, and surgery in particular, that he even requested in 1899 the following:

'Some day I shall have a tombstone put over me and an inscription upon it. I want only one thing recorded upon it, and that is to the effect that 'he laboured to divert his profession from the blundering which has resulted from the performance of experiments on the sub-human groups of animal life, in the hope that they would shed light on the aberrant physiology of the human groups'. Such experiments have never succeeded and never can'.[209]

A similar condemnation of a more particular form of vivisection was penned by Sir Frederick Treves, the famous surgeon, who, as reported in the *British Medical Journal* of 5 November 1898, declared:

'Dr. Halstead expresses his conviction 'that there should be a law compelling all surgeons to practice on animals the operations for circular suture of the intestines and for intestinal anastomosis'. I hope this view will not commend itself to the legislators of this country. Many years ago I carried out on the Continent sundry operations on the intestines of dogs, but such are the differences between the canine and the human bowel, that when I came to operate upon man I found I was much hampered by my new experience — that I had everything to unlearn and that my experiments had done little but unfit me to deal with the human intestine'.[210]

Of course it is obvious to anyone who has an iota of common sense that the tissues and precise anatomy of dogs and other animals are so different from those of humans that training up surgeons upon them is utterly ridiculous. A more recent surgeon, Dr. Leopold Zemann of Vienna, wrote in 1985:

'... I am of the view that no animal experiments whatever are ethically, morally or scientifically justifiable ... As Director of the Research Institute for Orthopaedics, I am able to report from many years' experience that all the developments of this kind in medical technique can be tested on humans themselves without animal experiments, without any injury to them'.[211]

Finally, we might quote the surgeon, Dr. Moneim Fadali, who likewise in 1985 wrote:

'Learning surgical technique by practicing on live animals is unnecessary, imprudent, cruel and unjustifiable. It has never produced a great surgeon. Practice surgery on live animals has been illegal in Great Britain since 1876, yet there is no indication that British surgeons are in any way inferior ...
Animal models differ from their human counterparts. Conclusions drawn from animal research when applied to human disease are likely to delay progress, mislead and do harm to the patient'.[212]

Even a child could understand this — that is, until the vivisectionists transform natural commonsense into brainwashed deludedness by their media-promoted propaganda. It is time for medical students and the general public to assert their native intelligence and not slavishly follow a tradition that would have us believe that mice are miniature men. They are not. Animals are not even dependable models for other animal species, or even for other individuals of the same species when placed in the highly artificial setting of a laboratory for the artificial introduction into their bodies of manifold maladies. Any deductions drawn from such experiments will be far, far less reliable than a British weather forecast of 30 years ago — and who amongst us would wish to stake our life on that?!

Infectious diseases
The claim that vaccination (the harmful progeny of vivisection) was the great force for good that swept away infectious diseases from our land is so histor-

ically inaccurate that we will give little space to it. Anyone who wishes to have their eyes opened to the health-damage wrought by vaccination should read Neil Z. Miller's excellent books, *Vaccines: Are They Really Safe and Effective?* and *Immunization: Theory vs. Reality* (New Atlantean Press, 1992 and 1996 respectively). Furthermore, dog researcher Catherine O'Driscoll of the Canine Health Census has amassed evidence that indicates vaccines are also harming the immune systems of the nation's dogs. Suffice it to say here that the *human* infectious diseases were already in definite decline *before* the introduction of the various vaccines and that it was because of better *accommodation, improved sanitation, hygiene and nutrition* that such diseases were pushed back. Introducing disease poisons, mucus, pus, cancerogenic formaldehyde, toxic thimerosal (a mercury derivative) and aluminium phosphate directly into the bloodstream and thus bypassing important parts of the immune system (which is what happens in vaccination) is contrary to all the laws of hygiene and rational medical practice.

Many decades ago, Benjamin Ward Richardson in his book, *The Health of Nations*, correctly credited one man in England with much of the health improvements that the nineteenth century brought with it: that man was the great hygienist and social reformer, Edwin Chadwick. Richardson wrote:

> 'By common consent Mr. Chadwick is esteemed as the designer of that modern sanitary science which has worked in the course of half a century such marvels for the prevention of disease'.[213]

These 'marvels' were accomplished by such simple measures as the removal of noxious refuse from houses, streets, and from the roads by sewerage; by increasing the supplies of running water; and by the employment of roadsweepers. Chadwick insisted that impure water was the source of much ill-health, including dysentery, and his views were backed up subsequently by doctors who confirmed that by draining the marshes of England, for instance, there was achieved a radical reduction in malaria and rheumatism. Chadwick also recognised the importance of fresh, clean, unvitiated air — a view with which the reader (living in a polluted twenty-first century world) will readily agree.

Diabetes and the discovery of insulin

Probably the favourite 'proof' amongst the votaries of vivisection for the efficacy and value of their sacrificial cult is the research into diabetes which, they say, culminated in the release of insulin for use by human diabetics. The vivisectors never tire of trumpeting this around as their great triumph. Unfortunately the historical facts are against them.

Diabetes mellitus (to give it its full Latin name, which literally means 'sweet siphon') is a disorder in which sugar and starch in the body are not oxidised to produce energy, due to a lack of the pancreatic hormone, insulin. One sign of this is that unhealthily high levels of sugar can accumulate in the blood and urine.

As early as 1766, Dr. Matthew Dobson noted (from his observations of *human* patients) that the urine of diabetics is loaded with sugar. Some twenty-two years later, in 1788, Dr. Thomas Cawley deduced through autopsy study a causal link between a damaged pancreas and the condition of diabetes — and this of course without any animal experiments. Unfortunately, these valuable insights were wasted throughout the nineteenth century, when vivisectors tried to produce diabetes in animals by damaging their pancreas glands. As Dr. Vernon Coleman writes, they '… failed miserably to get any useful, practical or relevant results'[214] which would progress medical understanding further than Dobson and Cawley had already advanced it. The nineteenth century's leading vivisector, Claude Bernard, actually came to the erroneous view that diabetes was a 'nervous ailment' (Hans Ruesch, *Slaughter of the Innocent*, p.212) and other vivisectors, basing themselves on Bernard's animal experiments, thought diabetes might be due to liver damage (M. Bliss, *The Discovery of Insulin*, Chicago 1982, p.209).

In 1833, however, the American military surgeon, Dr. William Beaumont, described the functions of the pancreas, not only in its exocrine function *vis à vis* the intestine for purposes of digestion, but also in regard to its significance for sugar metabolism, without, it is true, Dr. Beaumont's being cognizant of the precise hormonal basis of the process. All the valuable knowledge that Dr. Beaumont gained, however, was achieved by empirical observation of the war-wounded and by actually treating soldiers who had been injured in the upper abdominal area and the pancreas region. *Vivisection played no part in his discoveries whatsoever.*[215] Then in 1869, the researcher, Langerhans, discovered certain special cells (later named the 'islets of Langerhans') in rabbit pancreases which had lain in Mueller's solution. *This did not depend on vivisection*, since the animals could well have been dead before removal of their pancreases. In any case, analogous cells were later found in human beings.[216] Langerhans did not know what the function of those cells were. Now we come to the interesting part.

In 1920 Dr. Moses Barron (himself a vivisector) carried out an autopsy on a dead *human* subject who had suffered from 'pancreatic lithiasis' (stones in the pancreas) and diabetes, and it was specifically through this *human* necropsy that Dr. Barron was able to confirm his suspicion that the 'islets of

Langerhans' were causatively involved in the genesis of diabetes. Dr. Barron writes:

'A disease which offers *exceptional* opportunity for the study of the microscopic changes in the pancreas, especially with reference to the relation of the islets to the acini and their ducts, is pancreatic lithiasis. I had the *good fortune* to encounter accidentally such a case *while doing routine autopsies*. The lesion, by its very nature, being of long standing, presents gradually progressive changes in the parenchyma [i.e. the functional part of the organ] *that could be obtained in no other way, not even by experimental ligation of the ducts in animals*'.[217] (Emphases added.)

What we have here is a vivisector admitting that a vital, unique opportunity for understanding the pancreas gland and diabetes was bequeathed him by chance — not by animal experiments, but by a *human* subject. It is as a result of this 'good fortune' that Dr. Barron was able to confirm his and others' suspicions '... that the islets secrete a hormone directly into the lymph or blood streams (internal secretion), which has a controlling power over carbohydrate metabolism.'[218] Then in 1922 Banting (inspired by reading Dr. Barron's paper) and Best entered the scene — the vivisectors' favourite heroes.

These two Canadian researchers took insulin-containing extracts from cattle pancreases and tested them out on depancreatized dogs. Similar experiments had already been performed by other vivisectors, but as the *British Medical Journal* admitted at the time:

'Earlier attempts at extraction from the pancreas of a hormone controlling carbohydrate metabolism had produced results too capricious and indefinite to carry conviction.'[219]

Another doctor of the day, Dr. P. J. Cammidge, remarked upon the disparity between what vivisectors had achieved in dogs (where pancreas extracts had lowered their blood-sugar levels) and the application of those findings to humans:

'... numerous attempts to apply this knowledge clinically to the treatment of diabetes have ultimately ended in failure ...'[220]

Yet another physician, this time Dr. Ffrangcon Roberts of Cambridge University, spoke of the dangers that had attended efforts to replicate animal findings regarding pancreas extracts in humans:

'Although diminution in the blood sugar of depancreatized dogs on administration of pancreatic extract had frequently been observed ... *no results of any value* had been obtained by this method in the treatment of *human diabetes*. On the contrary, it has been said that the administration of such extracts *to human beings is not unattended with danger*.[221] (Emphasis added.)

All this by way of a prelude, to indicate to the reader that previous vivisections of animals had proven useless and even dangerous when the same things were tried out on diabetic human beings. But what of the famed Banting and Best?

They used — quite wrong-headedly — an extract from *degenerated* (i.e. ligated) pancreas glands on their dogs, and assumed thereby to have inactivated an enzyme that was destroying the insulin. They were, in fact, wrong in their assumptions; and by ligating the pancreas they actually ran the risk of damaging the insulin-producing islet cells and thus reducing the insulin yield! Dr. Roberts indicated at the time that these experiments were so sloppy that they did not at all prove the superiority of degenerated over normal pancreas extract — rather the reverse.

Best was still a student at the time of the dog experiments — and it showed. Even his mentor, Banting, displayed somewhat incompetent research skills. For example, the pair could not even agree on the dose of degenerated pancreas that they had given to their pancreas-deprived dogs: their published paper says 4 c.cm at one moment, but their chart (in the same paper) says 5 c.cm.! A further internal contradiction in their write-up of the experiments is that at one point they speak of giving injections of degenerated pancreas to the dogs at 12 o'clock midday (after dosing them up on sugar), but in their chart from the same published paper they say the time was 2.00 p.m.! Dr. Roberts, with commendable incisiveness and common sense, points out such errors (later essentially acknowledged even by a medical supporter of Banting and Best).

Dr. Roberts draws attention, for example, to these surprising time inconsistencies and other disturbing elements in the Banting and Best experiments. Here is a sample of what Dr. Roberts writes — in connection with what happened to the dogs' blood sugar levels after those dogs had been given doses of sugar. As indicated, there is a discrepancy between what Banting and Best's chart shows and what their text states, and this does not escape the careful eye of Dr. Roberts:

'The discrepancy here is important, for if the chart is correct the [blood] sugar had begun to return to its previous level before the sugar was given; if the text is correct the rise in blood sugar is at least partly due to the sugar given. With three subsequent injections of degenerated pancreas the blood sugar remained at about 0.20. Of the 20 grams injected only 0.21 was recovered in the urine. But there was practically no urine and the animal was dead next day. Truly, as the authors admit, no conclusions can be drawn from a moribund animal. The experiment only indicates that the degenerated pancreas lowered the blood sugar temporarily'.[222]

The same thing had already been achieved with 'normal' pancreatic extract by other experimenters. This was nothing new. Subsequent experiments by Banting and Best, where the dogs did not die, also only indicated that with very large and frequent doses of degenerated pancreas the blood sugar would temporarily fall, but that with moderately large doses the blood sugar was not reduced. Again, nothing excitingly new in this. Dr. Roberts points out various inaccuracies and ineptitudes enshrined in these Banting and Best experiments, including startlingly wrong interpretations of raw data, unsubstantiated claims, inequality of dosage for comparison, and a total lack of adequate blood-sugar fluctuation records after removal of dogs' pancreases but before administration of the extract. Dr. Roberts concludes his scathing attack on these two vivisectors by saying:

'The conclusion we come to ... is this: the production of insulin originated in a *wrongly conceived, wrongly conducted, and wrongly interpreted series of experiments.* Through *gross misreading of these experiments* interest in the pancreatic carbohydrate function has been revived, with the result that apparently beneficial results have been obtained in certain cases of human diabetes. Whether insulin will fulfil its promise time alone will show ...' [223] (Emphasis added.)

What is crucial to an understanding of the release of insulin into the therapeutic world generally is that this only became possible after J. B. Collip, Banting and Best's colleague, *purified* the insulin extract using *test-tube techniques,*[224] thus making it more acceptable to the human body. The original pancreas extract that Banting and Best had used in their dogs had proven ultimately *unsatisfactory* and literally useless in the first human patient (a 14-year-old boy, Leonard Thompson) whom it was tried out on, since it '... was found to cause a certain degree of local irritation', according to the head of Banting and Best's laboratory, Professor J. J. R. Macleod.[225] In fact, so severe was that local irritation that the treatment had to be stopped. The insulin preparation could not be used in that form. No less a person than Collip himself wrote of the original Banting and Best insulin preparation that it was '... *absolutely useless for continued administration to the human subject*' (Bliss, p.113, emphases added). That is why Collip had to try to purify this crushed pancreas extract. As mentioned, this was done by purely chemical means, although Collip did, foolishly, test the resultant preparation on dogs, which method of course would be incapable of giving any reliable results for humans, since the dogs had already failed to display the local irritation which characterised the human reaction to the unpurified insulin in the first place. Nor could any other animal give reliable results for safe application to humans.

So all these dog experiments had taught medical science nothing dependable about human diabetes and its treatment. Banting and Best had blundered into a series of irrelevant tests, and only produced usable insulin when their colleague, Collip, purified the degenerated pancreas extract using a technique of fractional precipitation with alcohol, and the resultant insulin preparation was then tested out on a diabetic colleague of Banting and Best — a certain Dr. Gilchrist. All the previous expenditure of time, money and animals in the vivisection realm had been utterly wasted, since the tests had proven inconclusive and, indeed, misleading.

Heart research

Heart disease is the biggest killer in the United Kingdom and America, soon perhaps to be overtaken by cancer. Vivisectors have been 'researching' human heart problems by rummaging around in the inner anatomies of rabbits, rats, dogs and other creatures for decades. Yet the results have been pitifully meagre.

The prevention of heart disease has long been known to be achievable largely by encouraging people not to smoke or become obese; to eat a vegetarian — or better still, vegan — diet, or at least to limit the intake of animal-derived fats; to reduce stress levels, and to take regular, gentle exercise. But the vivisectors continue wasting valuable time and resources by artificially damaging the arteries of rabbits, etc. in a vain hope of learning anything reliable or relevant about humans who spontaneously fall sick with heart disease after probably years of dietary and other self-abuse.

The problem has been neatly put by the vivisector, Professor John Martin, who specialises in heart research:

'If heart disease develops in a man or woman over 10, 20, 30 years, how am I to understand that and stop it in the beginning unless I have some way of studying it in the laboratory over a short time?'[226]

That is just the point: one cannot sensibly regard a different animal species that does not normally develop human forms of heart disease in the first place as a human model, and then try to speed up the whole process within a handful of months or years. Biological systems are not clockwork mechanisms or video films that can be 'fast-forwarded'. Such occludedness of vision as displayed by the vivisectors is bound to lead to ultimate failure. Professor Martin himself, after some 15 years of vivisection in the heart research field, has at least the honesty to admit that he has been a failure:

'I have not succeeded ...'![227]

This is Professor Martin's own verdict upon his attempts to find, through vivisecting animals, the cause of human heart attacks. Why has he failed in his avowed aim? The Professor himself gives us a vital clue to the mystery:

'We are dealing with human biology, *which is unpredictable*'.[228] (Emphasis added.)

Yes! Human biology cannot be predicted like a sequence of traffic lights or the following of dusk by dawn. Least of all can human biology be predicted by animals. Professor Martin really ought to know this but he carries on down the same old beaten path to inevitable failure. Perhaps he will one day listen to his own words and stop his laboratory irrelevancies with animals, for as he himself proclaims:

'The human species is *different from all other species*'.[229] (Emphasis added.)

How true that is. It is the essence of this book, and it is the reason why vivisection is always a foolhardy and potentially dangerous practice to perpetuate, fund and support. In the lottery of vivisection only the vivisectors and their paymasters win — the rest of us ultimately lose hands down.

If we wish to cast a glance in the direction of specific instances of vivisectionist heart research, we might care to look at some heart drugs and see what their relation to vivisection is. The following information is largely drawn from an excellent book by the veterinary surgeon, Brandon Reines.

The idea that cocaine could be used as a drug against cardiac arrhythmias (deviations from the normal beating rhythm of the heart) derived from human observations stretching back for centuries. In 1880, one of the vivisectionist investigators into cocaine and its effects upon the heart, von Anrep, admitted:

'I have had the intention after the study of the physiological effects of cocaine on animals also to make experiments on man. Other engagements until now have prevented me from doing so, *and the animal experiments do not permit practical conclusions*.[230] (Emphasis added.)

One of the main treatments used in recent years for the improving of angina pectoris (chronic chest pain) is the drug, nitroglycerin. Of this, Brandon Reines writes:

'The entire scientific development of nitroglycerin for the treatment of angina depended on direct clinical observations, which is now well-accepted. It was later shown that contrary to the animal test results, nitrite compounds do not lower blood pressure in human beings'.[231]

Antihypertensive drugs (drugs to bring down blood pressure) were overwhelmingly found useful through experience with human patients, not through animal research. It was attentive *clinical* observation which led Dr. B. Pritchard to recommend that 'beta blockers' be used to treat high blood pressure in humans. Another specialist in this area, Dr. Desmond Fitzgerald, confirms this:

'Pritchard's tenacious studies on the hypotensive action of propranolol eventually paved the way for the extensive use of beta blockers in hypertension even though this therapeutic application was not predicted from animal studies.'[232]

If we come to the question of artificial heart valves, the historical record is not as clear-cut as the vivisectors like to pretend. For years animal experimenters tried to test out various kinds of artificial heart valves in animals (notably dogs), including flap valves of diverse materials, ball valves, and homologous aortic valves:[233] but problems of fixing the device securely and with valve function, and especially with the dogs' tendency to develop thrombi (blood clots) which would block up the prosthesis and result in the dogs' deaths, made these experiments unsuccessful. Despite this, early satisfactory results were obtained in some human patients, although survival of those patients was limited to only a few months.[234] Nevertheless, the vivisectors, Starr and Edwards, continued to use dogs, and eventually came up with an artificial caged ball-valve that worked better in their animals than previous models had. What is interesting, however, is that they were simply unable to predict from their animal data whether this valve would prove viable long-term in humans, confessing:

'... there will remain uncertainty regarding the long-term wearing ability of a prosthesis' [i.e. in humans][235] and warning of possible unknown dangers (always the situation when one attempts to extrapolate procedures from animals to humans):

'... the advantages of the prosthesis over plastic procedures on the mitral valve in terms of predictability of hemodynamic result must be balanced by the *unknown long-term hazards* involved in total dependence upon an intracardiac appliance'.[236] (Emphasis added.)

When Starr and Edwards, buoyed up by their successes with dogs, came to try out their device on eight human patients, they nevertheless had to face up to the loss of two of those patients and serious complications in two others following the insertion of the new Teflon-cloth-utilising artificial valves. They of course (perhaps rightly) put these deaths and other problems down to situations unrelated to the new valves. But even in the other patients, problems occurred: some days after the operation, the vivisectors found that it was 'not unusual'[237] for patients to display congestive failure as manifested by enlargement of their livers and a greater tenderness in that region — *side-effects not noted by these researchers in their dogs*. Ironically, the drug which they chose to use to treat this problem successfully was digitalis, the very drug which vivisectors had years before warned *against* in humans (quite erroneously) because of its dangerous effects upon *dogs!* Starr and Edwards were equally in the dark when it came to the question of giving their heart valve patients anti-coagulant drugs: some of their dogs required anti-coagulant treatment, others did not. So the vivisectors plumped for giving this 'treatment' to their human patients without knowing whether it was useless or even harmful. Potentially hazardous guesswork, if ever there was any! As it turns out, humans *do* require anti-coagulants after receiving artificial heart-valves — yet we note that some of the experimental dogs did *not!*

When Starr and Edwards came to discuss their work with other vivisectors, the latter were very surprised by the former's relative success. Dr. George H. A. Clowes, Jr., praised Starr and Edwards' work, but raised the highly pertinent point of species differences:

'... lots of competent people ... have worked on it [i.e. artificial heart valves]. They found that the great problem was not that they could not put in valves that would work, but that they always produced thrombi in dogs ...

For that reason, many of us have been very reticent about putting in [into humans] these artificial protheses [sic] ... but Dr. Starr has ... proved the point that was brought out at the NIH [National Institutes of

Health] meeting in Chicago last fall concerning artificial heart valves, that probably *man does not react as violently as the animal does in producing a clot* at the interference between myocardium and the artificial prosthesis. It may be that *man is a better candidate for this type of thing than the animal*'.[238] (Emphasis added.)

Starr and Edwards subsequently (in the *Journal of Thoracic and Cardiovascular Surgery* 1961, vol. 42, pp. 673-682) confirmed that this was correct, stating:

'... the marked propensity of the dog to thrombotic occlusion or massive embolization from a mitral prosthesis is *not shared by the human being*.' (Emphasis added.)

Dr. Starr also revealed, most interestingly and intriguingly, that:

'The valve that we currently us [sic] in the dog *is somewhat different from the ball valve in the human*'.[239] (Emphasis added.)

So we have implicit here the admission that dogs, because of their differences, require a different type of artificial valve from humans. If the vivisectors are not comparing like with like (and clearly they are not), what was the point of all those dog experiments for medical application to human beings? Obviously, they were meaningless.

We could subject numerous other vivisectional claims to this kind of scrutiny, but we must press on. The key point always to remember is that no matter how many animal experiments are performed with a new drug or new procedure, the experimenter never knows in advance whether the human will react in the same way as the test-animals. The first human patients are thus always the true research 'guinea-pigs' in these situations. This leads us, rather neatly, directly into the nightmarish world of non-consensual *human* experimentation. But before we delve into those devilish realms, let us enjoy a little cultural interlude.

CHAPTER TEN

A Cultural Interlude:
Shakespeare and Wagner —
The Anti-Vivisectionists

L et us, in our imagination, step into a time machine and journey back to the England of nearly 400 years ago, for it is one of the best kept secrets of literary and cultural history that William Shakespeare (1564-1616), arguably the world's greatest ever dramatist, spoke out towards the end of his life against vivisection, which he did through the medium of his play, *Cymbeline* (written around 1610). If science had listened to his wise words on this, as on so much else, our society would not be in the state of moral and physical sickness under the weight of which it is groaning today.

What does Shakespeare have to say on the subject of animal experimentation? The answer is given in the Fifth Scene of *Cymbeline's* First Act, where the evil, scheming Queen (who wants to murder her son's rival to the English throne) approaches the court physician, Dr. Cornelius, for some 'drugs' which she says she wants to test out on animals to discover their effects. I shall quote the relevant section of the scene 'in extenso':

> *Queen:* Now, my master doctor, have you brought those drugs?
> *Cornelius:* Pleaseth your highness, ay: here they are madam:
> But I beseech your grace, without offence,
> My conscience bids me ask, — wherefore you have
> Commanded of me these most poisonous compounds,
> Which are the movers of a languishing death;
> But, though slow, deadly?
> *Queen:* I wonder, doctor,
> Thou ask'st me such a question. Have I not been
> Thy pupil long? Hast thou not learn'd me how
> To make perfumes? distil? preserve? yea, so
> That our great king himself doth woo me oft

For my confections? Having thus far proceeded, —
Unless thou think'st me devilish, — is't not meet
That I did amplify my judgement in
Other conclusions? I will try the forces
Of these thy compounds on such creatures as
We count not worth the hanging, — but none human, —
To try the vigour of them, and apply
Allayments to their act; and by them gather
Their several virtues and effects.
Cornelius: Your highness
Shall from this practice but make hard your heart:
Besides, the seeing these effects will be
Both noisome and infectious.

Let us now translate this into modern English!

The Queen has asked Dr. Cornelius for certain dangerous potions, but the Doctor suspects her motives (that she is plotting a murder), and the Queen notices this. She tries to pacify Dr. Cornelius by saying that she is not going to use these drugs on humans but only on animals, to see what harm they do and then to try to undo or halt the damage. The implication is that she wishes to gain 'knowledge' (Dr. Cornelius confirms precisely this in Act V Scene 5), which knowledge she then plans to apply to people. But does Dr. Cornelius, like our present-day vivisectionist 'researchers', say 'Fine! Go ahead with your valuable experiments'? Not a bit of it! He roundly condemns the whole enterprise on both *moral and scientific grounds*, saying it will harden the Queen's heart. Let us look first at the moral dimension of the Doctor's words.

The good Dr. Cornelius had only ever instructed his student, the Queen, in harmless pursuits, such as making perfumes (without performing animal tests!), extracting the essence of plants, and preserving food and fruits. But now the Queen is proposing to go one step further — into the 'devilish' realms of vivisecting creatures that, at that time, society considered 'vile' and 'of no esteem' (V/5), just as vivisectionists today try to claim experimentation on rats and mice as legitimate by viewing the latter as mere 'vermin'. But true scientists — as Hans Ruesch has memorably pointed out — recognise that the search for scientific and medical truth cannot be advanced by those who employ callous and hard-hearted methods in their research. Hans Ruesch quotes the great Sir Charles Bell, discoverer of the double action of the spinal nerves, who said: 'I don't think that men capable of such cruelties (i.e. those of vivisection) have the faculties to penetrate the mysteries of nature'.[240] Dr. Cornelius would have agreed with him.

Most revealing, furthermore, are the Doctor's words as he takes leave of the Queen. He mutters to himself: 'I do suspect you, madam; But you shall do no harm'. He is here saying that he will not allow the vivisection-mad Queen to harm either beast or person. These words issuing from a doctor's lips are no accident. They articulate the primary teaching of the great Greek physician, Hippocrates, whose oath doctors for many centuries were encouraged to abide by: 'Primum, non nocere' — 'First, do no harm'. The vivisector, however, always does harm! Hippocrates, by contrast, knew that the notion of curing disease by deliberately inflicting disease was a nonsense. Not once in his long life of nearly a hundred years did this most famous of all physicians ever condone or perform animal experiments (although the later Greek, Galen, indulged in the practice, much to medical posterity's grave harm). Shakespeare's exemplary doctor, Cornelius, like his spiritual mentor, rejects all vivisectionist practices.

Turning now to the scientific aspect of Shakespeare's attack on vivisection, we have to recognise the all-importance of a seemingly humble little adverb which Shakespeare slips onto the lips of his doctor-character — the word 'but':

'Your highness
Shall from this practice *but* make hard your heart'.

The word 'but' in this context has the meaning of 'only', 'do no more than', so that we might paraphrase the sentence as:

'By experimenting on animals,
The only thing you will achieve is that you will make yourself
    callous and hard-hearted —
You will achieve nothing else'.

In other words, she will *not gain any useful, relevant scientific knowledge*! Poisoning animals can never be used as a safe guide for poisoning human beings (which is what the Queen really wants to do — and Cornelius knows it), still less for finding ways of benefiting people (which is what she cunningly and mendaciously tries to imply she wants to do). Along with Dr. Cornelius (in a slightly different referential context) we might say that she like all vivisectors is being fooled by false appearances and unreliable results:

'She is fool'd
With a most false effect!' (I/5)

The whole drama is, in fact, concerned with the stark contrast between the appearance of things and the hidden reality underlying them, and with the operations of the Moral Law within human society. If the reader doubts that Shakespeare is linking vivisectional cruelty with other forms of human cruelty and mental unbalance, or thinks that maybe the Queen is not to be perceived as quite so evil after all, that reader should turn to the end of the drama, where Dr. Cornelius, in a kind of Greek choric comment, reports on the Queen's premature death from inward frustration at failing in her murderous plans, and where the good Doctor sums up the Queen's misguided life and resultant death in the following all-encapsulating words:

Cymbeline: How ended she (i.e. How did the Queen die?)?
Cornelius: With horror, madly dying, like her life,
Which, being cruel to the world, concluded
Most cruel to herself. (V/5)

Such transgression against the Moral Law as the Queen is guilty of inevitably brings suffering and disaster in its wake. Hans Ruesch makes an interesting point in connection with this Moral Law:

'The reasonings of the vivisectionists are un-scientific because they don't take into account the intangible realities of life. The Moral Law is one such intangible reality: And it is the incomprehension of this reality that marks the inescapable failure of experimental science when applied to living beings, with its inevitable sequence of tragic errors.'[241]

The wholeness of body and mind in integrated harmony, which is 'health', and the resultant peace which flows from it (the last word of Shakespeare's play is, significantly, 'peace'), can never be secured by vivisection, which even physically endangers the vivisector her/himself, as Shakespeare points out: carrying out experiments on animals is both 'noisome' (i.e. harmful, noxious, disgusting), he says, and 'infectious', i.e. can infect the vivisector with moral turpitude and actual disease, as Dr. Vernon Coleman has interestingly revealed:

'There is now clear evidence that people who perform animal experiments are exposing themselves to danger. A recent report in *JAMA* described an outbreak of lymphocytic choriomeningitis among laboratory workers handling mice or mice tissues. There have been a number of sarcomas and lymphomas at the Institut Pasteur in Paris where a survey showed an increase in the number of deaths from cancers of the bone, pancreas and brain among laboratory workers. And a report in *The Lancet* mentioned malignant melanomas and cancers of the blood as well as an increased risk of cancers of the brain and nervous system and stomach lining among laboratory staff'.[242]

Vivisection equals infection and disease indeed. How scientifically perceptive and accurate Dr. Cornelius (and behind him, Shakespeare) truly was!

A final interesting sidelight is thrown by the foregoing analysis on the vexed question of who in fact wrote the Shakespeare plays: some eccentric commentators have claimed that the real author was Sir Francis Bacon, the 'scientific' philosopher — a most bizarre assertion. Quite apart from the distinct differences of style between these two contemporaneous writers, there is another, for us even more compelling, piece of evidence against this claim: Bacon would appear to have been a supporter of torture and animal experimentation![243] Whoever wrote *Cymbeline*, it surely was not such a man. It was Shakespeare himself — literature's highest creative genius, whom we may also legitimately claim as one of the earliest and greatest protestors against the obscene and unscientific cult of animal experimentation.

Wagner

Jumping into our time-machine once again and zooming forwards by more than two centuries we arrive in a different land — Germany — and in the company of a different genius, the highly original and unsurpassed operatic composer, Richard Wagner (1813-1883). Although his views on race are unacceptable today, his understanding of the principles involved in the vivisection question was and still is second to none. Like Shakespeare, Wagner was appalled by the cruelty (he felt enormous compassion for the tortured animals, and indeed specifically identified his deep capacity for compassion as the presumptive wellspring of his art), but he was also cognizant of the medical lunacy represented by vivisection. He first heard about it from Ernst von Weber, the head of a German animal protection society, in 1879, when von Weber visited the great composer at his home, 'Wahnfried', in Bayreuth, Germany, and showed Wagner descriptions and depictions of what vivisection actually involved. Wagner was extremely distressed by what he learnt and suffered many bad dreams in consequence. Yet so strongly did he feel it his duty as a human being and an artist to oppose this evil that he resolved to write an article on the subject which could be prepared for mass distribution (at Wagner's own expense) — even though his wife, Cosima, did her best to stop Wagner from thinking about the subject at all, since it disturbed him so greatly.

Wagner wrote an 'Open Letter to Mr. Ernst von Weber', in which he spoke not only about the moral imperative of opposing vivisection, but also about its medical uselessness. He says that this kind of destructive 'science' (and he himself puts the term 'science' in inverted commas) is demonic and opposed to the dictates of common sense. The arguments of the vivisectors that their work is useful he dismisses as 'erroneous' (*irrig*), if not downright 'deceitful' (*trügerisch*);[244] indeed, he fulminates against vivisectionist medicine as being 'open poison' (*offenliegendes Gift*)[245] and states quite bluntly that vivisectional medicine is not science at all but the province of cowardly, fame-craving 'speculating'[246] physiologists. Wagner does not hesitate to say that he regards such people as quacks, bunglers or botchers (*Pfuscher*) in their profession, clambering about the tree of knowledge like lying apes, fearful that their lies will be found out, to whom he would not entrust his health and life.[247] He again dismisses as a mere vapid phantom (*Gespenst*)[248] the notion of vivisection's having any medical value and insists once more that animal experiments are useless, misleading and plain idiotic (*unnütz, trügerisch* and *stupid*).[249]

Wagner urges his readers to oppose vivisection root and branch — to demand its *absolute abolition* (as we do), not just its restriction or limitation. He says there can be no question of asking merely for reduction. Like the later Dr. Hadwen, he does *not* clamour for the development of 'alternatives' to vivisection: the system itself is so flawed, useless, misleading and rotten it must be done away with immediately and completely.

At the end of his little treatise, Wagner predicts that if vivisection is not soon destroyed, the next category of beings to become its victims will be *human* beings themselves.[250] Just how perceptive and far-sighted he was in this will be demonstrated by our next chapter.

CHAPTER ELEVEN

Human Experimentation

The coarsening of the sensibilities and the diminution in compassion and fellow-feeling which the practice of vivisection inevitably engenders (as Shakespeare pointed out) paves the mental way for vivisectors to consider, and perform, non-consensual *human* experimentation.

The high priest of nineteenthth-century vivisection in France, Claude Bernard, actually advocated the '... vivisection of human beings as the ultimate goal of experimental medicine', and in 1892, just a decade or so after Wagner's prediction of vivisectional experiments upon human beings, Lord Lister, the vivisectionist surgeon whose 'carbolic spray' to kill germs during surgery proved to be a killer of patients too, stated that it was 'a serious thing to experiment on the lives of our fellow-men, but I believe the time has now come when it may be tried'.[251]

Of course experiments upon humans without their knowledge or consent had already been going on for years. A certain Dr. de Watteville had published a letter in the *Standard* of 24 November 1883 (the year of Wagner's death) entitled 'The Use of Hospital Patients', in which he strongly urges that moral and monetary support should not be withheld from those hospitals which use their patients for purposes other than remedial treatment — i.e. for experimentation. This is the natural outcome of the vivisectionist attitude, which regards anything and anyone that is weak and powerless as 'fair game' for the experimenter's unbridled curiosity. In the *British Medical Journal* of 29 August 1891 mention is made of the experiments performed by a certain doctor who removed cancerous matter from the one infected breast of a woman patient and put it back, deliberately, into the other healthy breast to see what would happen.

As vivisection has flourished upon animals, so has a preparedness to experiment upon humanity itself. It is a psychological truth which all of us can surely verify from our own experience that the more one does a certain thing, the more used to it one tends to become. Thus the choking down of conscience as animals struggle to escape the vivisector's grasp and whimper in fear and suffering under the experimenter's sickness-disseminating syringe or merciless knife, gradually inures the experimenter to the notion of its being legitimate to inflict harm upon those entrusted to his/her 'care'.

In Tuskegee, Alabama, USA, starting in 1932 and going on for some 40 years, white racist 'scientists' decided to see what would happen if they intentionally left black males suffering from syphilis untreated as part of an 'experiment'.[252] The black victims were not informed that they had syphilis, still less offered the new treatments that were becoming available. To the experimenters these persons were just 'materials' to be played around with — just as earlier in the present book we heard one vivisector referring to how his colleagues 'play games' by giving cancer to mice and rabbits. Compassion for that which can *feel* should be indivisible. Sadly, when compassion is once lacking in one area of life it will usually wither away in another.

If I might add a personal reminiscence here, I am reminded of the time some years ago when I was working as a copy editor and translator for one of Europe's biggest scientific publishing houses. A female colleague with whom I shared my office was married to a vivisector, and she told me one day of how when her sister had suffered the trauma of a miscarriage and was distraught over the loss of the baby, the vivisector husband had simply not been able to see 'what all the fuss was about — she can always have another one', he had said coldly. No empathy. No ability to break out of the confines of self and identify with the suffering of another being. Such desensitization to the feelings of others is chilling.

This brings us directly to the sphere of babies and foetuses, and what is done to them in the name of 'science' or commerce. Professor Pietro Croce, the ex-vivisector, reveals what has taken place. Foetuses, he says,

'... are removed from the womb of the mother to be deep frozen or preserved in formalin or even, while still alive, decapitated, cut into pieces, ground into pulp, spun by centrifugal force and pressed to extract 'the juice' from them'.[253]

Another friend and colleague of mine suffered a late spontaneous abortion whilst in hospital four or five years ago — only to witness her live deformed baby being taken away from her by hospital doctors who said they wanted to 'study' it. Her blood ran chill.

There is hard, published evidence of experimentation upon aborted embryos from as recently as 1989 in connection with the terrible Thalidomide drug: in this particular study, done in Japan and supported by a grant from the New York Association for Aid of Crippled Children, scientists took four-

week-old embryos from healthy mothers through the collaborating obstetri-
cians. What happened next?

'These embryos were either intact with amnion, or partially damaged
without amnion. The upper limb buds [i.e. *arms*] were carefully *dissected*
from the embryos'.[254] (Emphasis added.)

Those nascent arms were then grown in culture for four days, and some
were exposed to the drug Thalidomide, while others were used as 'controls'.
They were then subjected to detailed microscopic analysis to see what effect
the Thalidomide had upon these little excised arm-buds.

Nazi and Japanese human vivisection practices in World War II

The experiments upon humans of all ages carried out by Nazi and Japanese
vivisection-trained 'doctors' and researchers in the Second World War are
notorious, and we need not tarry too long over them here. Dr. Annette Tuffs
actually states: '... it is now known that almost *half* of German doctors were
members of the Nazi party and, more significantly, many must have been
aware of the murders of 80,000 mentally ill people and the sterilisation of
thousands — or *were even involved*.' (Emphasis added.) (*The Lancet*, 2.11.96,
p.1234.) In fact, membership of the Nazi party and the 'SS' was far higher in
percentage terms among doctors than any other profession (*The Lancet*,
14.12.96, p.1662).

Examples of Japanese vivisectionist atrocities would include the following:
during the 1940s, the Japanese performed enforced experiments upon humans
suffering from frostbite and other effects of exposure to low temperatures.
According to Professor Tatao Matsumura of Keio University in Tokyo, 'Unit
731' in Harbin, NE China (which was the largest of a network of biological
warfare units) also carried out 'field-tests' in 1940, in which a plague
epidemic was deliberately unleashed upon the Chinese people of Manchuria
and claimed several hundred victims. This was only the first of such 'trials'.
According to Dr. Masataka Mori, a similar test took place in Congshan
village, near Yivu City in September 1942, with the result that 386 villagers
died. Two months later a Japanese biological warfare team arrived, burned
the village to the ground and took survivors to Linshan temple 3 km away for
vivisection experiments...[255]

Interfering with minds and brains

Around this same time, vivisectors in Europe and America were removing the
frontal lobes of chimpanzees (this in 1935) and felt that the animals seemed
more contented afterwards. Since then, on the basis of those animal experi-

ments, thousands of patients have had their frontal lobes surgically separated from the rest of the brain and the operation has been performed (doubtless without fully informed consent on the part of all the patients) for a ridiculously wide range of conditions. Dr. Vernon Coleman lists them: schizophrenia, depression, obsessional neurosis, anxiety, hysteria, eczema, asthma, chronic rheumatism, anorexia nervosa, ulcerative colitis, tuberculosis, hypertension, angina, cancer pain and — drug side-effects![256]

Even today in America, as a result of 'de-aggression' experiments performed on monkeys, certain politicians are suggesting giving extra serotonin to blacks and others viewed as violent or criminal to make them 'more passive'.[257] The equation is implicitly racist, as well as being socio-medically inept. Monkeys = men (especially blacks), the 'scientists' seem to be telling the gullible politicians. For example, the vivisector, Dr. Stephen Suomi of America's National Institute of Child Health and Human Development, says that monkeys with low levels of the brain neuro-transmitter, serotonin, display '... inappropriate aggressive behaviour ... they do stupid things that other monkeys would not normally do, for example dangerous leaping from the top of one tree to another ...'[258] Perhaps Dr. Suomi thinks that by giving blacks serotonin he will stop them behaving like stupid monkeys and leaping from one tree-top to another! How ridiculous. As even he himself has to admit, 'monkeys are not furry little humans with tails ...'[259] But of course that does not stop him and other experimenters extrapolating data from monkeys as though they were human.

One American scientist has some wise words in connection with dosing up poor, dissident youth with serotonin. Dr. Robert Murray of Howard University rightly reminds us of recent medical history:

'People have forgotten already that not too long ago, in the early '70s, people proposed not that low serotonin was the problem, but that there were misconnections in the brain and if we only zapped those connections that we could improve these kids' behaviour, and of course in some cases it did: they weren't violent any more — *they were just like vegetables*'.[260] (Emphasis added.)

As we are now in the area of mental health and vivisectionist medicine, let us hear what one of the leaders of Britain's mental health associations has to say about the 'side-effects' of drugs given to mentally sick patients. Judi Clements of MIND reveals the following:

'Our research shows that *over 60%* of people taking neuroleptic drugs experience *severe* or *very severe adverse effects*'.[261] (Emphasis added.)

The experience of a black man in Britain

An appalling example of the damaging effects of vivisection-based drugs for mental problems was provided in the mid-1990s by one of their victims, Mr. John Baptist of London. He is a young (around 30), intelligent, articulate Ghanaian black man who happens to believe that he is related to the Queen and that he was originally born white, with his skin later changing colour to become black. Idiosyncratic beliefs, to be sure, yet hardly likely to destabilise society or endanger his neighbours. Yet despite the fact that doctors confessed he posed no threat to himself or others, he was dragged off and 'sectioned' (forcibly detained in hospital) because of his 'inappropriate beliefs', as one 'care-worker' called them (shades of Orwell's 'thought police' here).

The consultant psychiatrist (doubtless raised on text-books replete with vivisectional data) who took charge of John's case during his sectioning was Professor Tom Burns of Springfield Hospital. Despite John's reiterated insistence that he did not want to take any drugs, since he had been damaged by them before, Professor Burns overrode John's heartfelt request and resolved to give them to him nonetheless, telling his staff:

'If he says no [i.e. to taking medication], then we should ensure that he is *injected this afternoon*'.[262] (Emphasis added.)

Does this show respect for the human individual and his powerless protests? The vivisectionist text-books which Professor Burns studied as a student would perhaps have made it clear that the resistance of laboratory animals during vivisection is to be overridden by using restraining devices and applying needles filled with narcotics. Is there not a link here to the human patient?

Professor Burns does in fact routinely give benzodiazepines (tranquillizers) along with other mind-altering drugs to his patients, and he does this for a particular reason:

'It generates a little bit of retrograde amnesia, so often the patient doesn't remember the rather *undignified tussle* that's involved in giving him an injection'.[263] (Emphasis added.)

So the Professor is prepared to have his staff grapple with John, a peaceful, harmless soul, to force 'medication' upon him against his express wishes. That medicine must be extraordinarily beneficial! It must make the patient feel on top of the world and glowing with health if the Professor needs to administer it in this manner! Actually, all is not sweetness and light with the medication in question, as even Professor Burns has to admit:

'The main problems [i.e. of side-effects from the mind-medication] are either a stiffness and a sluggishness, as if the limbs are heavy; they [i.e. the patients] walk slowly with a rather shuffling gate, *a bit like people with Parkinson's disease*. More distressing is a restlessness, where the patients ... cannot keep still'.[264] (Emphases added.)

Most of us think of medicine (quite wrongly, in the case of 'orthodox' medicine) as a healthy thing, as something which will do our body and mind a power of good. But what do we have here? 'Medicine' which causes in the taker symptoms comparable to those of Parkinson's disease! Is this what vivisectional medicine has come to? It is. And we might note in passing that many drugs that are said to alleviate mental problems, especially the symptoms of 'depression' in animals, do not have the same effect on depressed or stressed humans, as the psychiatrist, Dr. J. Steven Richardson, confirms:

'... behavioral improvement [i.e. in 'depressed' animals] is ... typically produced by a wide range of drugs that are *not effective in treating depression in people*'. (Emphasis added.) (From *Progress in Catecholamine Research*, Alan R. Liss 1988, p.231.)

Furthermore, using the results of animal tests to determine safe/effective dosage levels of psychotropic (mood-altering) drugs in humans is, in the words of a vivisector, Dr. R. W. Brimblecombe, quite valueless:

'Our results are *absolutely valueless* for predicting dose ...' (*Chemical Influences on Behaviour*, ed. Porter and Birch; Churchill 1970, p.193. Emphases added.)

Animal data can also be seriously misleading in that they indicate danger where there is in fact relative safety and value. Epileptics, for instance, are sometimes given anti-convulsant drugs to alleviate the convulsive fits into which they can fall. One such drug is phenobarbital ('phenobarbitone' in Britain). Dr. J. Clemmesen writes:

'In recent years, so-called evidence [he is referring to vivisectional evidence] to the carcinogenicity of the well-served anticonvulsant phenobarbital has been presented, based on mice predisposed to liver tumors, and rats responding in some experiments with benign growths. Had it not been for its merit phenobarbital might well have been prohibited on the basis of such reports, *without regard to their lack of conclusiveness in man*'. (Emphasis added.) (Coulston and Shubik, op. cit., p.263.)

Yet phenobarbital can produce, amongst other symptoms, diffused pain, dizziness, headache and hangover in the human patient (*MIMS*, February 1996, and *ABPI Data Sheet Compendium*, 1991-2). How could we expect a rat or a mouse to tell us if it feels dizzy, or has a hangover?

But let us return to John and hear his own testimony as to how the medication previously prescribed to him wrought rather less than desirable changes in his psyche and soma. He tells of how he was:

'... injected in my private parts secretly and it kept out of my files. I came out of this hospital hardly able to brush my teeth — hardly able to eat — hardly able to stand ... *I was less than a baby. What sort of medicine is that?* You keep me here by force, and drug me so much that I cannot even get out of the hospital on my own ... *What sort of medical practice is that?*'[265]

Why, vivisectional practice, of course. It is the inevitable outcome of a system of medical training that brainwashes the students into believing that the *feelings* of the weak and powerless are of no account, that they can be ridden roughshod all over, that animals and people are not individuals, filled with the capacity for suffering as well as joy. Even our old vivisectionist friend from a previous chapter, Dr. Frederick Coulston, comments on this:

'We should go back to the old days when we looked at animals as individuals as one would look at a patient in a hospital ... Parenthetically, some people who are now treated as patients in hospitals also have the feeling that perhaps they are not treated quite the way they would have been a few years ago'.[266]

Many patients complain about the cold, unfeeling way they are treated by some doctors. This is the inevitable outgrowth of a 'modern' medical system that long ago sanctioned heartlessness and callousness in a large segment of its less than humane research methodology. The soul of vivisectionist medicine is perverted and blood-stained. It is time for medicine to return again to the sane and sound principles of inner and outer hygiene and health propounded over 2,000 years ago by the unsurpassed physician, Hippocrates — as the wise and good Dr. Hadwen urged at the beginning of the twentieth century. Yet precious few have heeded his words.

Human vivisection in China and vaccine experiments on soldiers

Needless to say, the vivisectionist mentality has not only taken hold of our Western medical practitioners, but has extended itself even as far as China — China, where the famed Dr. Li of many centuries ago brought Chinese medicine to great heights *without a single vivisection* but by experimenting upon himself and carefully observing his patients. Now, however, we are confronted with the appalling situation of Chinese prisoners being hurriedly sentenced to death so that *their organs can be immediately extracted by 'doctors' and sold to rich buyers for transplants.*[267] Some prisoners have *still been fully alive while both their kidneys were being removed* ...

The horror is too great and we must pull back.

The litany of non-consensual experimentation upon humans could, however, be extended to the cocktails of vaccines and drugs given without adequate explanation or consent to soldiers sent off to fight in the Gulf War of 1991, only for thousands of them to return crippled, or fatally ill, or with deformed babies — all the effects of Gulf War Syndrome, created by their 'protective' (animal-tested) medication. But we must now call a halt and return to where we began: with the animals themselves.

CHAPTER TWELVE

Resting Our Case

The reader who has followed us this far will, I believe, be clear that the halting of vivisection does not mean the halting of medical progress. We can think of few more telling admissions on this subject than that of Dr. Mark Matfield, Executive Director of the Research Defence Society — the organisation set up by vivisectors to defend themselves and their industry.

The intriguing admissions of Dr. Mark Matfield

In the summer of 1995 an anti-vivisectionist wrote to Dr. Matfield, putting forward the view that medical progress would have been and still can be achieved without the use of animals. Dr. Matfield's reply was unexpected:

> '*I am sure it could be.* In fact, many areas of medical research do not use animals at all'.[268] (Emphasis added.)

These are the words of a man who is paid to insist that vivisection is vital to medical progress; a man who earns his living by trying to justify and defend what his confrères get up to in the vivisection laboratories. Yet here he comes clean and says, essentially, that animal tests are *not* necessary for the advancement of medicine. Admittedly he later adds the rider that progress would be 'fairly limited' (only 'fairly', we note), but he has nevertheless conceded the central point that advancement could be secured without the use of a single animal.

The perceptive reader will of course have realised by now that it is actually not a question of whether the abolition of vivisection would damage medical progress or not, but whether in all conscience and common sense we can afford (financially and health-wise) to continue along this meandering and nebulous path of animal experimentation when the results are so meaningless because so inconclusive and even tragically misleading. Human health would in fact be the winner if the irrelevancies of the vivisection method were ended this minute — and we now register with delighted surprise Europe's leading vivisectionist, Dr. Mark Matfield himself, making a significant step towards acknowledging that medical progress would not be suspended if vivisection were terminated today.

Let us stay with Dr. Matfield for a page or two longer since he has further revelations to make. In the same letter already quoted from, he admits that animal experiments *'do not tell us exactly what goes on in the human system'* (emphasis added) and refers to the only sensible way of learning about human disease, which is 'clinical research', both upon healthy and sick, fully consenting, fully informed *volunteers*:

'This is the *gold standard*, since here we learn what *really* happens in *humans*'. (Emphasis added.)

We must attend carefully to Dr. Matfield's words and imagery here: the 'gold standard' is a system where the value of a currency is defined in terms of gold, where gold is the highest and solely relevant determinant of monetary worth, against which currency may be exchanged. If a person were to come along and want to buy a product (priced according to the gold standard) using an irrelevant and inferior standard (say, the 'copper standard'), he would be laughed out of court as a joker. And so it is here: anything less than the study of humans for an understanding of humans is an inferior and irrelevant standard, for which no valuable information will be exchanged. Dr. Matfield confirms the illusory nature of the results of animal experiments by saying that human clinical research tells us what *'really'* happens in humans — in other words, animal tests do *not*. They deal in imaginary and fictitious scenarios only.

This fascinating and informative letter concludes with its author's agreeing with his correspondent that 'prevention is much better than cure' in the field of human health, and citing the example of how people should eschew cigarette-smoking — smoking, the very cause of human cancer *which animal experiments have signally failed conclusively to demonstrate*! Dr. J. Clemmesen writes in this connection:

'For decades the clinical [i.e. human] observation of an association between cigarette smoking and bronchial carcinoma [i.e. lung cancer] was subject to unfounded doubt, suspicion, and outright opposition, largely *because the disease had no counterpart in mice*. There seemed to be no end of statisticians craving for more documentation, *all resulting in fateful delay of needed legislative initiative*'. (Emphasis added.) (Coulston and Shubik, op. cit., p.263.)

Think of how many untold thousands may have died as a result of animal-based assurances that smoking was 'safe'...

Reverting to Dr. Matfield and his eye-opening admissions, we should like to refer to another letter from him[269] where he comments on a survey carried out by Dr. Vernon Coleman, in which 88% of some 500 doctors surveyed agreed with Dr. Coleman that 'laboratory experiments performed on animals can be misleading because of anatomical and physiological differences between animals and humans'. What was Dr. Matfield's own response to this proposition?

'I would certainly agree with that. Of course they *can* be misleading. If you choose the wrong animal model you will get the wrong answer.'

Needless to say, Dr. Matfield has deftly dodged the crucial question here, namely: how does one know whether one has the right or wrong animal 'model' *until one has subsequently tested out the new medication or procedure on a human being to ascertain retrospectively the relevance of the results gained from the animal?* One simply cannot know in advance whether there will be any correlation between the animal reaction and the later human one. Even the famous scientist, Sir Ernst Boris Chain, Nobel Prize winner, celebrated for his co-discovery with Florey (and Fleming) of the anti-bacterial effects of penicillin, stated under oath before a court of law investigating the Thalidomide tragedy:

'No animal experiment with a medicament, even if it is carried out on several animal species *including primates* under all conceivable conditions, can give any guarantee that the medicament tested in this way will behave the same in humans; *because in many respects the human is not the same as the animal!*[270] (Emphasis added.)

Dr. Matfield gave voice to similar sentiments when he appeared on national radio in 1994 and spoke about detecting drug 'side-effects' during animal and human tests. This is what he said:

'Any new drug goes through animal testing and then it goes through clinical testing on humans, and *it is the clinical testing,* as it's called — testing on human volunteers, first healthy human volunteers with very tiny amounts of the drug, and then moving on to human volunteers with the disease in question — *that's where you'll pick up the side effects; that's where you'll find out whether it is going to work. Surely'.*[271] (Emphases added.)

We could not have put it better ourselves. We might add that were it not for those mandatory clinical trials (which, as we have seen, are far, far fewer than the animal tests) the number of drug disasters would be considerably greater.

More blunders from the RDS

The Vivisection Defence Society (sorry, 'Research Defence Society'!) has some odd members and collaborators, people who seem ill-versed in even the basics of biology. Some of their vivisection-supporting statements are hilarious in their ineptitude. For instance, Mr. Simon Brophy, who runs the Biomedical Research Education Trust (an offshoot of the RDS), dismissed as 'completely untrue' my 100% accurate statement on radio that animals are genetically different from people.[272] When we consider that it is differences in genes which determine, amongst other things, the anatomy and morphology of our bodies, if what Simon Brophy claimed were correct we could expect to see him sitting at his desk with, for example, a humming-bird's head and beak on top of a giraffe's neck, growing out of a wart-hog's body supported by a millipede's 'thousand feet'! Mr. Brophy also attempted to dismiss my examples of species differences regarding strychnine, death cap toadstools and arsenic toleration in animals and people as 'silly' and 'foolish' — overlooking the fact that my data were drawn from the vivisectors' own experiments!

This brings us to the oft-remarked phenomenon of the vivisectors' inability to agree about what their experiments tell them. The case of penicillin illustrates this quite well. It has long been known amongst vets that guinea-pigs and hamsters are particularly sensitive to penicillin. In fact, penicillin is contraindicated (warned against) in these species because it can kill them relatively easily. Dr. Matfield agrees and says:

> 'The guinea-pig, almost uniquely, is the one animal if you give penicillin to it, it develops a fatal case of enteritis'.[273]

One researcher Dr. Green carried out a study in 1974 in which he revealed that penicillin activates a latent virus in both guinea-pigs and hamsters. Yet Dr. Jack Botting of the RDS says:

> 'There is no basis for citing the effect of penicillin on guinea-pigs as a prime example of species difference'.[274]

Yet his own boss, Dr. Matfield, goes on national radio and does precisely that. I suppose the two vivisectionists were looking at different sets of vivisection results!

Another member of the RDS — its Honorary Secretary, no less — has voiced in the closed and secretive world of the vivisectors his own view that animal models in asthma research (his specialist area) are less than dependable. Writing in a medical journal on 'airways hyperresponsiveness' (AHR) in the asthmatic patient, Professor Clive Page states:

'Established clinically efficacious antiasthma drugs ... will often atten-
uate this acute AHR, although novel therapeutic agents which
demonstrate this same property in animals *may not neccessarily* [sic!] *show
clinical value in man*'.[275] (Emphasis added.)

Professor Page, who on another occasion described vivisection as 'an
imperfect science',[276] concludes his little paper with the words:

'In conclusion, at present *there is no ideal animal model of chronic asthma*
and such a seemingly *complex disorder may be impossible to mimic* [i.e. in
animals]'.[277] (Emphasis added.)

This obsession with using animals to try to mimic human ailments really
is quite ludicrous: the comedian/impersonator, Rory Bremner, can mimic the
Prime Minister of Britain splendidly but that does not make him the actual
Prime Minister, able to determine national policy or predict the PM's next and
every move, any more than the artificially created 'similar' symptoms of an
animal malady, while 'mimicking' the human illness, are reliably predictive
of *the spontaneously developed illness in man*. Sometimes I think that the vivisectors have missed their true vocation as side-splitting comics!

An associated vivisector colleague of Professor Page's who shares his views
on animal 'models' and human asthma is Dr. K. F. Chung. Reiterating
Professor Page's point that bronchial asthma is a complex disease, Dr. Chung
correctly states:

'Animal models *have fallen short of reproducing the human disease*, particularly in mimicking the spontaneous and persistent airflow obstruction
that characterizes asthma'.[278] (Emphasis added.)

A vet speaks out

Trying to find drugs to treat asthma by using animals who do not suffer from
asthma is just one more example of vivisectionist illogicality. Even vets (sadly
by and large part of the vivisectionist drug Establishment) are now beginning
to speak out against animal tests. Here is what veterinary surgeon, Richard
Allport, MRCVS, writes:

'The many drug tragedies, such as thalidomide, show that the results of
animal experiments are not necessarily going to give us safe drugs. It is
not wise — or even in my view scientifically valid — to extrapolate the
results of animal testing into the human field. There are many therapies
— such as Homoeopathy and Acupuncture — which make the search
for new drugs unnecessary.' (Letter to the author, 31.5.95).

In veterinary medicine itself, vivisection is ethically unacceptable and can be medically misleading, since artificially induced maladies in laboratory creatures are an unreliable guide to the symptomatology and cure-potential of spontaneously sick wild or pet animals. The vivisection laboratory exposes the animal to all manner of fears and stresses which in themselves can invalidate the experiments. Moreover, deliberately taking a healthy animal and inflicting disease upon it is both morally unpardonable and medically redundant: there are already enough naturally diseased animals around to try out sensible treatments upon *in the interests of the individual animals themselves.* Richard Allport rightly reminds his veterinary colleagues that vivisection is incompatible with their duties and responsibilities as animal carers:

> 'I would urge all veterinary surgeons involved in any way in animal experimentation to search their consciences, and remember the oath they took on becoming a member of the Royal College of Veterinary Surgeons: "My constant endeavour will be to ensure the welfare of animals committed to my care". *This to me means having no involvement with vivisection'.* (Ibid.)

Why do vivisectors continue with their useless work?

Returning to the human field, the reader may well be wondering why vivisectors continue to use a method that has failed so signally and so appallingly. The answer is simple — MONEY. Money, careerism, varying degrees of sadism, lack of originality of thought — and (as a consequence) the blind, unthinking following of historical tradition. One vivisector, Dr. J.M. Manson, when asked why certain species were used in vivisection and not others, replied: 'At this point, it's *historical*' (emphasis added) (this is in the 1987 book *Developmental Toxicology*, ed. by J. Mclachlan, R. Pratt and C. Markert). Vivisecting animals is indeed historical — an historical *error*. Using animals in 'research' is a traditional, easy and lucrative way of earning a living and advancing one's career by, for example, publishing 'scientific' papers — albeit one may find oneself admitting in them that one's work 'has fallen short' of what is medically required truly to benefit humankind. Vivisection also provides a convenient alibi in a court of law when chemical manufacturers are faced with the human health damage they have caused: 'We tested our product on animals and it seemed safe. We are not to blame if humans didn't imitate the animals' reactions as we had hoped ...' Drug companies whose chemicals have maimed and killed have successfully escaped harsh penalties by essentially using this plea.

Even those who are no longer active vivisectors, but who sit behind desks or go on radio and television defending vivisection, can earn a comfortable living doing so. The yearly salaries (or 'staff costs') of the little coterie of workers in the RDS came to £204,745 in 1993 and only slightly less, at £189,807, in 1994.[279] And as far as we have been able to ascertain, the regular daily staff members in the RDS office in London number scarcely more than three persons, with the cheery, chatty, bouncy Dr. Mark Matfield at their head. As one famous TV character would say, promoting vivisection is 'a nice little earner'.

Just in case the reader is wondering, *no one* at UKAVIS (*UK Anti-Vivisection Information Service*), which was founded by this author, is paid even one penny for the hours and months and years of work they devote to this slow but steady campaign of national education: we work for truth, not profit.

Speaking of profit

Speaking of profit: if one is the head of a giant drug company (and these are amongst the richest organisations in the world), or an industrial chemical manufacturer, one of the best ways to get dangerous products onto the market is to use the 'Lethal Dose 50%' (LD_{50}) animal test, to 'prove' the safety limits of one's product for human beings. We have seen how variable diverse animal species are, so virtually whatever results one wishes for can be obtained. But even the pro-vivisectionists will admit that these acute or chronic toxicity tests are meaningless. The well-known (amongst chemical workers) pro-vivisection publication, *Croner's Substances Hazardous to Health*, says in its February 1987 edition (p.1-23) on the LD_{50} 'safety' test:

'Many problems exist with this method, including the fact that all animals, even within a species (e.g. different strains of rats), have variable metabolic pathways and different susceptibility to the effects of the same chemical. Therefore, *different laboratories working with the same breed of animal produce different LD_{50} results*. The antivivisection view that this method kills too many animals needlessly is not unreasonable ...' (Emphasis added.)

A little later on (p.1-25) we read:

'Despite the fact that animal tests often form the basis for legislative control measures it is important to remember, that *humans do not necessarily respond in the same way as animals* ...' (Emphasis *not* added.)

It is because they are aware of this fact that the giant Procter and Gamble chemical company as recently as 1995, after testing a synthetic musk fragrance on mice and obtaining liver tumours, dismissed such results as '… of little relevance to humans'. (*Ethical Consumer*, November/December 1995, p.24).

What is always omitted is that it was the vivisectionists themselves who lobbied for such tests to be enshrined in law — obviously because they knew that vivisection is a method so amenable to manipulation, so flexible, so malleable in the results it can deliver, that it gives the company 'scientist' the best possible opportunity to come up with whatever results his/her paymaster requires. Or to dismiss as irrelevant unfavourable results if and when they occur.

Other vivisectionists have admitted that they are having great 'problems' with the vivisection method. Professor Nick Wright of the Imperial Cancer Research Fund confessed to Dr. Vernon Coleman in a TV debate in 1992: 'I can tell you *large numbers of problems* with animal experimentation' (emphasis added), and others have admitted that the toxicity tests performed on animals are scientifically worthless. In 1977, Philip Rogers, Managing Director of Hazelton Laboratories (a vivisection establishment) had this to say:

> 'The LD_{50} is a crude measure of toxicology. There is really *little scientific justification for the test* because reproducibility is not good, *it can vary from day to day*, and the results *are dependent on the animal strain used*'. (Emphasis added.)

A few years earlier, the toxicology expert, the late Professor Gerhard Zbinden of the World Health Organization, stated:

> 'Most adverse reactions which occur in man *cannot be demonstrated, anticipated or avoided by the routine subacute and chronic* [animal] *toxicity experiment*'.[280] (Emphasis added.)

The fact is that, as we have seen with animal research into carcinogens, animal tests more often than not *come up with the wrong answer*. It is lunacy to place any faith in them. Even Dr. Ralph Heywood, past scientific director of the Huntingdon Research Centre (U.K.), another vivisection establishment, admitted in 1989:

> '… the best guess for the correlation of adverse reactions in man and animal toxicity data is *somewhere between 5% and 25%*'.[281]

This means that *up to 95% of the time, animal 'safety' tests deliver false results and thereby constitute a threat to human health, rather than a safeguarding of it.*

Testing for birth defects

Another area where vivisection is notably used to no sensible end is that of teratogenicity testing, that is to say, testing whether a chemical might cause birth defects in the offspring of the person who absorbs that chemical. Of 38 chemical compounds known to cause birth malformations in humans, only 45% of those chemicals caused damage in hamsters and a mere 30% caused birth defects in monkeys[282] (our 'all-but-identical' relatives). On the other hand, animal tests have told us that some 1,000 substances are teratogenic (productive of birth deformities), whereas in fact they have *not* been found to be so in humans.[283] No less a journal than *The Lancet* points out the inability of researchers to determine the relevancy of animal teratogenicity tests for the biologically different human being:

> 'When a new agent is marketed, its complete metabolism may not be fully understood. And, *how can one judge whether the teratological data obtained in animal species with different metabolic pathways are relevant to man?*' (*The Lancet*, 26.1.91. Emphasis added.)

How indeed?

As recently as 1996, *The Lancet* spoke of the misleading nature of vivisection in connection with the drug rifabutin, suspected of causing neutropenia (i.e. a reduction in the number of special white blood cells):

> 'To conclude, on the basis of animal studies, that rifabutin is safe and well tolerated in man, irrespective of whether neutropenia occurred in animals is misleading'. (Dr. Glen Apseloff et al., *The Lancet*, 7.12.96, p.1593.)

The same old story: animal tests giving misleading information.

Another prestigious medical publication, the *British Medical Journal*, in 1996 contained a letter from Dr. Gabriel Symonds, who clearly perceives the foolishness of vivisection, this time in connection with the alleged possible benefit of the Thalidomide drug to treat 'proliferative retinopathy' (a form of eye damage). Dr. Symonds quotes from another doctor:

> '... studies of Thalidomide in people with proliferative retinopathy are awaited, but animal studies have shown no benefit'.

Dr. Symonds then adds her own highly pertinent comment:

> 'If they [i.e. animal experiments] have shown no benefit then why go on to human studies? Or if animal studies are not relevant to human disease, then *why do them?*' (*BMJ*, 7.12.96, p. 1488. Emphases added.)

More and more doctors are evidently waking up to the utter futility and illogicality of the vivisectors' work.

Returning to the subject of teratogenicity: experimenters display a marked predilection for trying to induce birth defects in animals after they have already been observed in humans. Even one of the vivisectors involved in this kind of work recognises that to speak of 'predictions' in these circumstances is plain ridiculous. Dr. Hanson points out that looking for teratogenicity in animals *after it has already been demonstrated in people* is a nonsensical form of 'prediction':

> 'It seems to me that of some [sic!] teratogens seen in animals and humans were identified after the fact; that is, until somebody knew what to look for, they did not seek those things. To suggest that this process is predictive is somewhat of an anomaly in terms. *It can hardly be predictive after the fact*, if prediction implies that one looked and then predicted something, not that one saw something [i.e. in humans], *and then hunted until you found a system* [i.e. an animal] *that would predict it*'.[284] (Emphasis added.)

'Wisdom' after the event, and the aspartame conundrum

The reader will perhaps by now be gaining an insight into one of the practices that keep many of these experimenters busily in work: trying to find an animal 'model' or 'system' that will behave similarly to the human, when the human information is already long in. It is like saying, 'I can see that humans get indigestion if they consume large quantities of tough, wild grass, but I won't believe it until I've made an animal suffer the same gastric inconvenience'! The vivisector finds a glaringly obvious fact in the human sphere and then sets about trying to 'prove' it by creating a similar thing in the animal sphere. This is redundant 'wisdom', a shameless profligacy of time, valuable resources and lives. But of course it is a continuing source of profit for those involved in the experiments.

Dr. Hadwen wrote many years ago of the 'humour of the vivisector' — that is, of the experimenter's being involved in such a ludicrously silly system of research that one is tempted to believe that he/she is doing it all tongue-in-cheek out of a twisted sense of humour. An amusing example of vivisectional variation in the results obtained is provided by the food additive, aspartame. This chemical (used in some diet colas) was tested out on mice, rats and dogs. In the dogs there was a resultant weight *loss*. In the mice there was no effect on weight, except for a significant weight *gain* in the thyroid gland. And in rats, no effects were noted, except that aspartame made the male rats (not the females) more *hungry!*[285] Faced with this kind of conflicting data, Dave Hattan, one of the safety regulators at the U.S. Food and Drug Administration, responded that it '... only confirmed the need for testing on humans'.[286] The animal results were a useless chaos of unknown and unknowable possible significances and insignificances. Time and lives were (as always) sacrificed in vain.

What about transplants?

When the subject of vivisection is aired on radio or television, usually some pro-vivisectionist will cry out: 'What about transplants? They were only made possible through animal experimentation!' As so often, the facts, when studied carefully and intelligently, do not bear this out.

First of all, transplants are generally an admission of medical failure, in that doctors have allowed a heart or kidney or other organ to become so damaged that it is no longer within the realms of repair. Transplants are all too often a last-ditch attempt to salvage a human life from the shambles of failed medical treatment. In addition, the cost of transplants is so high that only a small proportion of people in the world could ever afford them.

Moreover, the success rate of transplants is not particularly high. The *Sunday Times* in 1995 carried a report that revealed that *one in five* human organ transplants are *rejected* by the patient, and only 50 or 60% of the transplants that 'take' last for five years.[287] The central problem with transplants is that of rejection, to prevent which drugs are given to suppress the immune system — the very system that protects us from disease.

Furthermore, disease can itself be transferred along with the donor organ. John Wallwork, the transplant surgeon at the Papworth Hospital in Cambridge, who is a co-founder of IMUTRAN, a company seeking to transplant animal organs into humans, has disclosed:

> 'I think we're very concerned about that, because one of the issues of transplantation from human to human is you actually transmit a lot of diseases, and we have no choice in that, because *it is a lottery*'.[288] (Emphasis added.)

Just like vivisection itself — a lottery, a game of chance. And as I write this, only today an Englishman who had a kidney transplant was reported as having gone down with cancer caused by disease latent in that very same donor kidney (*News at Ten*, 18.1.96). How much more risky will animal organ transplants into humans be, with the threat of unsuspected viruses entering the human system? More of this shortly.

Let us return to the animals: did they in fact make transplantation (such as it is) possible? Far from it. The simple fact is that animals are possessed of different immune systems from humans, so they respond differently from us to transplants. One cannot reliably extrapolate from animal results to human beings. Steve Beddard, in his fine book on the subject, makes the point very well:

'Experiments on animals will tell the researchers one thing only. It will tell them about animals; not about people. When the first human transplants were carried out, they were all to fail, because of the reliance on studies done on animals.'[289]

Hans Ruesch has revealed how the first heart transplant patients suffered greatly after the operations performed by Christian Barnard in his bid for fame. Hans Ruesch quotes from an article by Malcolm Muggeridge:

'At the end of eighteen days, he [Mr. Washkansky, the first heart-transplant patient] thankfully expired. "They're killing me," he managed to get out before he died. "I can't sleep, I can't eat, I can't do anything. They're at me all the time with pins and needles ... All day and all night. It's driving me crazy."'[290]

On the basis of this *human* experience, Barnard's next patient, Dr. Philip Blaiberg, managed to be kept alive for two years. But here too the suffering was considerable; as his daughter revealed:

'"I don't know if it was the drugs or the transplant, but he was a different man. Physically, my father's life was hell after the transplant. He was suffering terribly all the time, but he did not want the world to know this..."'[291]

Any subsequent success with transplants has come about through clinical experience, not animal experiments.

What about genetically engineered transplants? The same principle applies: an animal with a human gene stuck into it is still an animal, not a human. One swallow does not make a summer, nor does one human gene make a human being. As Professor Pietro Croce stated to me in personal conversation, a human gene inserted into an animal is still surrounded by a biological environment which is *animal* and thus able to exert an influence upon the expressive power of that gene which we cannot predict. Genes do not exist in blissful isolation; they are part of a web of complex interconnections and interactions which make up the supreme miracle of the human individual.

The results obtained from genetic manipulation or mutation in one living being may be markedly different from those obtained in another, as the geneticist, Professor Nick Hastie of Edinburgh University, rightly asserts:

> 'Genes do not work in isolation. Identical mutations may have *very different consequences in different individuals*.[292] (Emphasis added.)

Equally, the notion of eradicating illnesses by eradicating genes thought to cause those illnesses is reckless, simplistic science. Dr. William Cookson, a practising geneticist himself, wisely reminds us that:

> '... most of the genes that affect common diseases are *there for a reason* and that *genetic diversity is extremely important*, and ... manipulating these genes in some way or another could have *adverse effects which are not known about*, because no one has looked'.[293]

He also sensibly says:

> 'Labelling genes good or bad is to oversimplify our complex genetic make-up'.[294]

The geneticist vivisectors who think that they can dictate human biological destiny by fiddling around with the genes of animals are forgetting two things: firstly, that (as the Israeli veterinary surgeon, Dr André Menache, wrote in personal correspondence to me last year) 'animals are lousy models of human diseases' — with or without a human gene stuck into them; and secondly, that genes are not miniature despots that sway the fate of entire biological systems in utter isolation: they *interact with, and are modified in their effects by, an environment, both biological and social.*

Animal-to-human transplants

The reader will have heard of the research company, IMUTRAN, and its attempts to transplant genetically modified pigs' hearts into cynomolgus monkeys. The foreign hearts were inserted into the abdomens of the hapless monkeys, but *those hearts were not sustaining the life of the recipient monkeys* — that function was still being performed by the creatures' original hearts: the pig hearts were simply beating to no useful purpose.

Even so, the hapless monkeys only survived, on average, for a pathetic *40 days*.[295] On the basis of these meagre results the experimenters are 'hopeful about creating the same effect in man'.[296] They wanted to start human clinical trials on five or six patients needing heart or kidney transplants in 1996, but as this book goes to press in 1997 there has been no news of any such successful operations having been performed. Certainly one fears for the well-being of those first 'human guinea-pigs' when and if the operation eventually goes ahead...

The research journalist, Robbert Matthews, writing in the *Independent on Sunday* of 17 September 1995, has some revealing and sensible comments to make on this whole scenario of bits of pigs going into monkeys and humans:

> 'First, to ensure that the DNA is copied into as many of the pig's cells as possible, the swapped DNA must be inserted into the pig very early in the life well before it is born. But in experiments, scientists have had problems getting all of the DNA to function correctly in all of the organs.
>
> Second, even if the genetically engineered organs do succeed in fooling the human's immune system for days, or perhaps weeks, combating longer-term rejection is likely to prove very tricky. Even entirely human organs put into patients whose immune systems have been chemically suppressed mysteriously fall prey to such problems ...
>
> In 1993, a team at Cedar-Sinai Hospital in Los Angeles attempted to transplant a pig's liver into a 26-year-old woman. With nothing to protect the organ from attack by her immune system, the patient was dead within a day.
>
> The scientists working on xenotransplantation [trans-species transplantation] know they are in a race to be the first to succeed with a human patient. *What they now have to decide is what they mean by "succeed"'*. (Emphasis added.)

And, as James Le Fanu, writing in the *Sunday Telegraph* of 17 September 1995, says in connection with these foreign transplants into monkeys:

> 'In the meantime, perhaps we should spare some sympathy for the unfortunate monkeys whose sacrifice at the moment seems *so purposeless'*. (Emphasis added.)

Most revealingly, an animal experimenter involved in genetic research himself has poured scepticism and scorn upon the alleged viability of xeno-transplantation (animal-to-human transplants). Dr. Michael Antoniou is a specialist in genetics at one of the world's leading medical research institutions in Britain, and he explains that the 'humanised' animal organs may be able to immobilise the body's rejection system for the first few hours (the 'hyperacute rejection' stage due to 'complement proteins' which circulate in the bloodstream of the patient and bind to foreign cells, causing their lysis, i.e.

destruction) — but long-term survival of the animal organ in its foreign human host is extremely unlikely. Dr. Antoniou comments that overcoming the initial 'hyperacute rejection' will yet '… do nothing for the subsequent antibody and T-cell mediated response'. (Letter to the author, 28.9.96). Powerful immunosuppressant drugs (which undermine the body's vital resistance to disease) will therefore have to be administered to the patient — but these are far from perfect in their action. Moreover, long-term use of such immunosuppressives is associated with such serious side-effects as renal toxicity, hypertension, diabetes, and cancer (Dr. Richard D. Granstein, *The Lancet*, 28.9.96, p. 838). 'What makes matters worse', adds Dr. Antoniou, 'in using animal rather than human organs, is that you cannot match "tissue types"'. As a consequence, if the animal organ is to have any chance of survival, it will need to be humanised still further with other proteins (called histocompatibility antigens) on the cell surface. But there are some 2,000 proteins on the cell surface, any one of which could trigger off an immune-system response! Dr. Antoniou's conclusion is emphatic:

> 'It is therefore *unreasonable to think we are on the brink of animal organ transplants*. Any transplant carried out now may survive the initial acute rejection period *but will certainly be rejected soon after* by antibody and T-cell activity … *From a scientific standpoint, what we read in the press would appear to be hype by the companies and clinicians involved*'. (Letter to the author, 28.9.96. Emphasis added.)

There is an even more worrying prospect: namely, that harmful animal viruses, undetected in the transplanted organ, will enter the patient's body along with the organ and later transmit themselves to other people who have close or intimate contact with that patient. After all, early in the 20th century the virus of 'swine influenza' from pigs caused the deaths of around *20 million people*. Vivisectors are now hoping to put pig organs into people. Even if they screen for known viruses, there is still a chance of unknown viruses getting through and wreaking havoc. Dr. Jonathan Allan, a virologist interested in baboons — another animal proposed by some for organ transplants — warns of the dangers (*Panorama*, BBC TV, 24.6.96):

> 'We are playing Russian roulette with introducing viruses into the human population'.

Even Dr. David White, the vivisector of the company IMUTRAN, who has bred 'humanised' transgenic pigs for xenotransplants into humans, has agreed that there is no way such an operation can be made completely safe until it is done ('We cannot know that there is no risk') and that what is proposed means '... putting at *unreasonable* risk those first few individuals who inevitably we will have to start with when we go into the clinic'. (*Panorama*, 24.6.96, emphasis added).

Dr. André Menache, President of Doctors and Lawyers for Responsible Medicine, is even more disturbed by the potential dangers for society of xeno-transplantation. In a public lecture in London in 1996, Dr. Menache warned that viruses which may lie latent in the animal organs (harmless to the animals) could become lethal in the new biological environment of a human being. They could mutate, combine with human viruses and become much more virulent — and could be spread by coughing, sneezing and sex, etc. And once a new virus is out into the community, stopping its potentially fatal spread could be all but impossible. Dr. Menache concludes:

'Animal-to-human organ transplantation is *far too risky a venture to which to subject the general population*, and as such *should be abandoned ...*'

BSE research

Also inappropriate are the current experiments being carried out on trans-genic mice (mice with a human gene inserted into them) to determine if BSE ('Mad Cow Disease') can be transmitted to humans. As the microbiologist, Professor Richard Lacey, said of these mice experiments in 1995:

'The experiments they are conducting are desperately artificial',[298]

and:

'These experiments tell us about the mouse, *not the man*'.[298]

Certain American and other vivisectors have proposed using chimpanzees in BSE research, but Professor Lacey is equally excoriating in his dismissal of this idea of feeding chimps BSE-infected material to see what will happen to them:

'It is completely hopeless. It is scientifically unjustified. *In fact, it is quite useless*'. (*Nothing but the Truth*, Channel 4, 27.10.96.)

Apart from the fact that the only relevant information is the epidemiolog-ical data coming in from already-infected humans, Professor Lacey is perhaps mindful of the situation of chimps' overwhelming refusal to contract AIDS when injected with HIV or of their failure to fall sick with Hepatitis when injected with the Hepatitis C virus! (See Professor Vernon Reynolds' fine book, *Poor Model Man: Experimenting on Chimpanzees*, 1995.) Even the normally vivisection-promoting British Government is apparently sceptical about the value of using chimpanzees in BSE research. In a letter to the author from Eleanor Bowden of the Ministry of Agriculture, Fisheries and Food, the British Government's position is made clear:

> 'We have had, and still do have, serious reservations about carrying out transmission work on chimpanzees, partly because *it will still not give a difinitive* [sic!] *assessment of risk to man*'. (Letter of 26.11.96, emphasis added.)

In other words, the ubiquitous vivisection problem is in evidence here too: what happens in animals (including chimps) has no reliable bearing on what might happen in humans.

We might add here that some vivisectors claim successfully to have transmitted Creutzfeld-Jakob Disease (the human equivalent of Mad Cow Disease) to transgenic mice, but all attempts to transmit a similar 'prion' disease (fatal familial insomnia) to normal laboratory animals, *including 18 primates* (our closest 'cousins'), have failed — despite the fact that it is known that *this disease can be transmitted to humans.*[299] Confusion upon confusion.

Wise words from a biologist on genetic engineering

Most sane people respond with horror when they see a mouse with a human ear grafted onto its back (as in recent American experiments). Such distortion of a living being's body reflects the distortion of the perpetrator's mind. These experiments are not only a violation of another creature, they are pointless (the 'ear' could not hear, and the mouse had no adequately functioning immune system, so it could not reject it) and they are also a violation of the human spirit. I should like to close this book with the wise words of Professor Mae-Wan Ho, biologist at the Open University in the UK. Writing initially on botanical genetic transfers, but using words that beautifully fit the situation of all genetic engineering, Professor Ho has the following to say:

> 'Genetic engineering is based on the key idea that the characteristics of organisms are determined uniquely by stable genes such that the transfer of the genes automatically results in the transfer of the desired characteristics. This is an extreme form of genetic determinism that has already been invalidated, *and rejected by most biologists. It has also been falsi-fied by gene transfer experiments themselves.*
>
> A whole complex of interactions occur between genes and cellular organisation, and between the organism and its environment in the development of all the characteristics of the organism. The conse-

quences of transferring foreign genes into organisms with a long evolutionary history of an integrated developmental system in a particular ecological community are hence *impossible to predict, especially in our present state of ignorance*.[300] (Emphasis added.)

Speaking of what we might call the vivisectionist-mechanistic vision of life which typifies the *Weltanschauung* of some biologists, Professor Ho perceptively links this mind-set with various forms of exploitation throughout the world:

'All that [i.e. Neo-Darwinism] is part and parcel of a reductionistic and competitive world view that sees societies as nothing but collections of isolated individuals driven by a desire for sex and for profit and who would lie and cheat at every turn. It is *anathema to all holistic ways of life*, especially among the indigenous peoples of the world, which have proven themselves to be sustainable, economically viable and effective in maintaining social and individual well-being.

The same reductionistic world view is the ideological backdrop to centuries of imperialistic colonisations and conquests, which transformed into the present era of economic exploitation under the monetary policies of Northern Governments and the multi-national monopolies. At the same time, it has effectively marginalised every alternative worldview and knowledge system and silenced all opposition on its way to homogenise all nations and cultures to the free-market model, which only deepens the dependence of the South on the North, serving to make the rich richer at the expense of the poor, the homeless and the hungry of both North and South'.[301] (Emphasis added)

The marginalisation of knowledge would include such health-practices as herbalism, homeopathy, acupuncture and naturopathy, which do not rest upon the rotten foundations of vivisectionism. In addition, genuine science can lead the way in the testing of new medications by utilising human cell cultures, tissue cultures and organ cultures, as well as 3-D computer modelling and by expanding the indispensable human volunteer trials which are ultimately the most reliable of all methods in the advancement of medical science. Above all, a massive reduction in the use of drugs should be advocated by the health professions and a return to natural, herbal and dietary, preventative and curative medicines, which are far less fraught with danger for the human body. But let us finish with Professor Ho's superlative insights, as she sums up the true nature of the genetic engineering bandwagon upon which so many dollar-hungry vivisectors are now trying to jump. Professor Ho reminds us that the genome of any being is not the be-all and end-all of that being — the genetic inheritance lives in mutual co-existence with a modifying *environment* — and the Professor concludes her article with the following observations:

> 'The collapse of the genetic paradigm has been known for at least the past 10 years. Yet the practitioners of neo-Darwinian evolutionary theory, like the New Biotechnology brigade, have uniformly failed to acknowledge this or to make it known to the public. The result is that *a gigantic hoax is being perpetuated*, comparable to the South Sea Bubble, on investors in biotechnology as well as on humanity at large with our common future at stake.
>
> There is no longer any vestige of justification for the reductionist world-view which has been thoroughly discredited on all fronts. *The long, unmitigated violence against the human spirit it inspires, the violation of nature and of life cannot be allowed to continue'*.[302] (Emphasis added.)

❀ ❀

Summation

You have now read of vivisection and the heartless, reductionist and illogical mentality that animates its practices. I hope that you are now persuaded of its medical pointlessness and dangers, or at the very least inclined to *question* the public propaganda constantly thrust upon us as to how valuable animal experiments are deemed to be. If you would like to help abolish this unscientific wrong against humanity and nature, this primitive practice that has no place whatever in twenty-first century medicine, then please inform yourself further by reading the books listed below and then inform others, especially your Member of Parliament, of the dangerously misleading nature of this outgrowth of nineteenth century mechanistic 'scientism'. If you truly care enough, about people, animals and the polluted planet (polluted by products passed as 'safe' through the vivisection laboratories), please make your views known in all available media newspapers, radio and television. Vivisection thrives on public ignorance. Help dispel that darkness, and take inspiration from such giants as the fearless and compassionate Dr. Walter Hadwen, who at the commencement of a new century still points our way out of the tenebrous gloom of pseudo-science — and into the redemptive light of human and humane scientific research and humanitarian modes of living.

If you are a science or medical student, you will require great courage to oppose the follies of the vivisection method, as there is nothing so dogged and bullnecked as academic conservatism — especially when it is defending a lucrative error. But true medical progress has always depended upon the *few*, who dare to speak out the truth. As an editorial in an anti-vivisection pamphlet endorsed by Dr. Hadwen stated some decades ago:

'To oppose vivisection, when every year seems to establish it more firmly as a State-supported, Press-advertised 'boon to humanity', requires *courage*. So does every advance that humanity has made. Those who uphold this practice thoughtlessly, because it is the 'proper thing' so to do, would equally, had they been born earlier, have supported the tortures of the Inquisition or negro slavery, and would, of course, have agreed with every dogma of medicine, however absurd or revolting, that belonged to the age in which they lived'.[303]

This 'Hadwenite' article then calls for pioneers (in medicine as in life), for those with the vision to see beyond the prejudices of the present time and traditions — '... those who have a more alert intelligence, greater courage and daring, and a higher ideal than the rank and file'.[304]

Dr. Hadwen himself (like Hans Ruesch much later in the century) sums up the way forward for all progressive people wishing to fight the unscientific and barbaric practice of vivisection in the following, stimulating words (spoken by his characters, Dr. Devereux and Dr. Deguerre, in his anti-vivisection novel):

'From my experience among medical men, I am fully convinced that, if ever the anti-vivisection cause is to succeed, anti-vivisectionists must be prepared to answer the stock medical arguments advanced on behalf of experiments on animals, and they must be prepared to weigh the subject historically and scientifically in all its bearings, and the man or woman who fails to do that must expect defeat. The moral aspect is, I admit, the highest ground that can be taken, but, as long as human nature remains what it is, it will never relinquish the claim that the strong are justified in benefiting at the expense of the weak; and anti-vivisectionists, to be successful, will have to wield the double-edged sword that not only presents the immorality of the practice, but also its stupidity and danger. The moral conscience is reached sooner by fear and ridicule than by high ideals unsupported by scientific facts ...
The best thing in life is, after all, to fight for a cause worth fighting for, and to fight thoroughly. It will lead us, I believe, to look back upon the past with satisfaction and to the future with confidence, and though the

battle be long and the forces against us many, we may rest assured that 'the race is not always to the swift nor the battle to the strong,' but that right and truth will eventually triumph. If we are to succeed we must deserve success, and the warrior who is to win his battle must allow no weak spot in the harness'. (*The Difficulties of Dr. Deguerre*, Dr. W. R. Hadwen, C.W. Daniel, 1926, p. 591.)

Are *you* prepared to be a peaceful fighter in this noble cause? Or do you prefer, sheepishly and blindly, to follow the herd into the abyss? The decision and its responsibility rests with you, as will the consequences. Let *wisdom* and *compassion* guide you in your choice. Please remember: the fate of animals and humankind lies truly (and ever will) in *your* hands ...

All creatures and all objects, in degree,
Are friends and patrons of humanity.
There are to whom the garden, grove, and field,
Perpetual lessons of forbearance yield;
Who would not lightly violate the grace
The lowliest flower possesses in its place;
Nor shorten the sweet life, too fugitive,
Which nothing less than Infinite Power could give.

William Wordsworth, *Humanity*, 1829

Highly Recommended Reading

SLAUGHTER OF THE INNOCENT by Hans Ruesch (CIVITAS 1983): the greatest presentation ever of the medical, moral and scientific case against vivisection. This book was responsible for inspiring a world-wide movement of doctors, scientists and others against vivisection. A powerfully written, highly informative, unique work. 446 pages. *PRICE: £6.95*

EXPERIMENTS ON LIVING ANIMALS: USELESS AND CRUEL by Dr. Walter R. Hadwen (originally published in 1914; projected UKAVIS re-publishing, 1997): A clear, well-argued and compelling essay by a medical doctor who was the first to stress the necessity of fighting vivisection scientifically. No British anti-vivisectionist medic has ever surpassed Dr. Hadwen in dedication to the anti-vivisection cause or in gaining the reputation for being 'unanswerable' when debating the vivisection question. Approximately 40 pages. *PRICE: £4.00*

NAKED EMPRESS or THE GREAT MEDICAL FRAUD by Hans Ruesch (CIVIS 1982): A very powerful book which exposes the harm to human patients which the vivisection methodology has caused through its erroneous results. The book also examines the tremendous vested interests that lie at the back of vivisection. 222 pages. *PRICE: £9.50*

1,000 DOCTORS (AND MANY MORE) AGAINST VIVISECTION by Hans Ruesch (CIVIS 1989): a fascinating collection of statements and testimonies by doctors and medical scientists as to the uselessness and dangers of vivisection, ranging from the 19th century to the penultimate decade of the 20th century. 281 pages. *PRICE: £10.00*

VIVISECTION OR SCIENCE: A CHOICE TO MAKE by Professor Pietro Croce (CIVIS 1991; translated by Henry Turtle from the Italian): A ground-breaking work, in that it represents the experience over many years of a vivisector who eventually renounced the practice on account of its medically misleading nature. Professor Croce (a respected doctor and pathologist) presents a mine of scientific information to discredit vivisection utterly. 230 pages. *PRICE: £7.00*

BETRAYAL OF TRUST by Dr. Vernon Coleman (European Medical Journal 1994): An extremely readable book on the harm that doctors do, the corrupt and ruthless pharmaceutical industry and the utter illogicality of the vivisectors and their methods. Dr. Coleman is himself a well-known medical doctor. 150 pages. *PRICE: £6.00*

FIGHTING FOR ANIMALS by Dr. Vernon Coleman (EMJ 1996): an inspiring collection of the author's views on vivisection, hunting and meat-eating. Written in a remarkably clear, personal style; a book that gives much food for thought. 143 pages. *PRICE: £9.95*

CAUGHT IN THE ACT: THE FELDBERG INVESTIGATION by Melody MacDonald

(Jon Carpenter 1994): a fascinating, harrowing account of the infiltration into a famous vivisector's laboratory in Britain in the late 1980s. Anyone who believes that vivisection is humane and scientific should read this book! 82 pages. *PRICE: £6.00* (NB: *UKAVIS* does not share the approach of all of the 'anti-vivisection' organisations mentioned in this otherwise very fine book).

CANCER, CURE AND COVER-UP by Patrick Rattigan, N.D. (NEMESIS 1993): a booklet that could help save lives, by exposing the dubious nature of orthodox cancer 'treatments', and which looks at more natural, alternative methods of prevention and cure. 24 pages. *PRICE: £2.50*

THE USE OF ANIMALS IN MEDICAL RESEARCH: THE WRONG PATH by Dr. Tony Page (UKAVIS 1996): A booklet aimed at teenagers, which presents a number of instances of 'species variations' and explains why vivisection cannot work, but why it is still carried on. Foreword by Professor Vernon Reynolds of Oxford University, and humorous illustrations by Carole Zdesar. 32 pages. *PRICE: £2.00*

All the above very useful works are available at the prices stated (which include p & p). Prices are correct at time of publication, but may vary without notice. Cheques should be made out to 'UKAVIS' and sent with your order to:

(UKAVIS) UK ANTI-VIVISECTION INFORMATION SERVICE
PO BOX 4746
LONDON SE11 4XF

Organisations

The Publisher can supply a list of British organisations dealing with 'green' and animal issues. Inclusion on the list does not necessarily imply endorsement or approval by the author of this book. For a copy please send two second class stamps to:

Jon Carpenter Publishing
The Spendlove Centre
Charlbury
Oxfordshire OX7 3PQ

Those in the USA or Australia who would like to contact genuine anti-vivisection organisations can write to the following voluntary, abolitionist groups:

SUPRESS
PO Box 10400
Glendale
CA 91209-3400
USA

GUARDIANS
PO Box 59
Pascoe Vale South
3044 Victoria
AUSTRALIA

References

1   H. Zangrossi, Jr., S.E. File, 'Habituation and generalization of phobic responses to cat odor', in *Brain Research Bulletin* 1994; 33: pp.189-194.

2   P.F. Watson, T.E. Glover, 'Vaginal anatomy of the domestic cat (Felis catus) in relation to copulation and artificial insemination', in *Journal of Reproduction and Fertility Supplement* 1993; 47: pp.355-359.

3   A.D. Le, Y. Israel, 'A simple technique for quantifying intoxication induced by low doses of ethanol', in *Pharmacology, Biochemistry and Behavior* 1994; 48: pp.229-234.

4   P. Sacra, N.B. Roberts, W.H. Taylor, 'Production of acute gastric erosions in the cat by individual human pepsins', in *Clinical Science* 1995;88: pp.47-50.

5   H. Tsuchiya, C.J. Bates, 'Ascorbic acid deficiency in guinea pigs: contrasting effects of tissue ascorbic acid depletion and of associated inanition on status indices related to collagen and Vitamin D', in *British Journal of Nutrition* 1994; 72: pp.745-752.

6   L. Watters, C.D. Hopper, T.J. Gruffydd-Jones, D.A. Harbour, 'Chronic gingivitis in a colony of cats infected with feline immunodeficiency virus and feline calicivirus', in *Veterinary Record* 1993; 132: pp.340-342.

7   Dr Philippe Shubik in *Human Epidemiology and Animal Laboratory Correlations in Chemical Carcinogenesis*, edited by Frederick Coulston and Philippe Shubik (Ablex, New Jersey 1980), p.123.

8   *Journal of Comparative and Physiological Psychology*, 22 January 1972, quoted by Hans Ruesch in *Slaughter of the Innocent* (CIVITAS 1983), p.139.

9   Ruesch, op. cit., p.136.

10 *Surgery, Gynecology and Obstetrics*, March 1968 quoted in Ruesch, op. cit., p.132

11 Quoted in *Why Animal Experiments Must Stop* (European Medical Journal, Second Edition, 1994) by Vernon Coleman, p.10.

12 Coleman, op. cit., pp.10-11.

13 Immanuel Kant, 'Beantwortung der Frage: Was ist Aufklaerung?' (1784); reprinted in *Was ist Aufklaerung?* (Reclam, Stuttgart 1974), p.9. Translated here by Dr. Tony Page.

14 We indirectly gleaned this interesting fact from *Why Are Animal Experiments Necessary?* (pamphlet of the pro-vivisection 'Biomedical Research Education Trust' 1994, p.1.

15 See Professor Pietro Croce's invaluable book, *Vivisection or Science: A Choice To Make* (CIVIS 1991, trans. by Henry Turtle), pp.31, 37 and 39.

16 *Multiple Sclerosis in Simple Terms*, booklet of the Multiple Sclerosis Society of Great Britain and Northern Ireland (1995), p.5.

17 Cf. Croce, op. cit., pp.22-24, for most of these and other examples, and also

Dr. Walter R. Hadwen's *The Difficulties of Dr. Deguerre* (Daniel, London 1926) (now sadly out of print), p.558.

18   C.D. Barnes and L.G. Eltherington, *Drug Dosage in Laboratory Animals A Handbook* (University of California Press, Berkeley and Los Angeles 1964), p.22.

19   Ibid. p.81.

20   Ibid. p.93.

21   Barnes and Eltherington.

22   Ibid.

23   Ibid. p.217.

24   Barnes and Eltherington.

25   Dr. Randall C. Baselt, *Disposition of Toxic Drugs and Chemicals in Man* (Biomedical Publications, Davis, California 22nd edition 1982), p.701.

26   Barnes and Eltherington.

27   Ibid. p.236.

28   Quoted in Ruesch, op. cit., p.364.

29   Barnes and Eltherington, p.110.

30   Dr. Colin P. Groves in *Comparative Primate Biology (Vol. 1): Systematics, Evolution, and Anatomy*, ed. by Daris R. Swindler and J. Erwin (Alan R. Liss, New York 1986), p.196.

31   All these orang examples are taken from Dr. Groves' chapter in Swindler and Erwin's above-mentioned work, p.197.

32   Ibid. p.199.

33   See Croce, op. cit., p.62.

34   Groves, op. cit., pp.202-203.

35   Dr. R .N. Short in 1980, quoted by Groves, op. cit., p.206.

36   Groves, op. cit., pp.212-216.

37   Stephen I. Helms Tillery, Timothy J. Ebner, John F. Soechting, 'Task dependence of primate arm postures', in *Experimental Brain Research* (Springer-Verlag, Berlin, Heidelberg, New York 1995, 104), p.11.

38   Michael Schultz, 'Forelimb of the Colobinae', in Swindler and Erwin, op. cit., p.649.

39   Schultz, p.650.

40   Ibid.

41   Ibid.

42   Ibid. p.651.

43   M. Katz and B.J. Poulsen, 'Absorption of Drugs through the Skin', in *Concepts in Biochemical Pharmacology* Part 1, ed. by B.B. Brodie and J.R Gillette (Springer-Verlag, Berlin, Heidelberg, New York 1971), p.111.

44   Katz and Poulsen, op. cit.

45   Ibid.

46   Ibid.

47   Ibid.

48   Ibid.

49   Ibid.

50   Dr. Jennifer S. Lund (ed.), *Sensory Processing in the Mammalian Brain: Neural Substrates and Experimental Strategies* (Oxford University Press 1989).

51   See Donald A. Wilson and Michael Leon, 'Information Processing in the Olfactory System', in Lund, op. cit.
52   James C. Boudreau, 'Analysis of Mammalian Peripheral Taste Systems', in Lund, p.23.
53   Ibid. p.31.
54   Ibid.
55   Ibid. p.40.
56   Ibid. p.41.
57   Dennis P. Phillips, 'The Neural Coding of Simple and Complex Sounds in the Auditory Cortex', in Lund, p.172.
58   Ibid.
59   See Markowitsch's chapter on the 'Prefrontal Cortex', in *Comparative Primate Biology (Vol.4). Neurosciences*, ed. by Horst D. Steklis and J. Erwin (Alan R. Liss, New York 1988), p.102.
60   See Steklis and Erwin, op. cit., p.73.
61   Ibid.
62   Markowitsch, in Steklis and Erwin, op. cit., p.103.
63   Dr. Simmons, in Steklis and Erwin, op. cit., p.196.
64   See Jon H. Kaas and Michael F. Huerta, 'The Subcortical Visual System of Primates', in Steklis and Erwin, op. cit., pp.327-391.
65   Kaas and Huerta, ibid. p.327.
66   See Dr. Rodieck, 'The Primate Retina', in Steklis and Erwin, p.267.
67   See Rodieck, for example, Ibid.
68   Ibid. p.264.
69   See Markowitsch, in Kaas and Huerta, op. cit., p.101.
70   Dr. Hepp Reymond, in Kaas and Huerta, op. cit., p.605.
71   Ibid.
72   Ibid. p.606.
73   See Dr. Horel, 'Limbic Neocortical Interrelations', in Kaas and Huerta, op. cit., pp.89,90,ff.
74   Markowitsch, in Kaas and Huerta, op. cit., p.128.
75   Dr. Eberhart, 'Hormones, the Brain, and Sexual Behaviour', in Kaas and Huerta, op. cit., p.694.
76   Ibid.
77   Ibid. p.695.
78   Ibid. p.696.
79   *The Rat in Laboratory Investigation*, ed. by Dr. Edmon J. Farris and Dr. John Q. Griffith, Jr. (JB Lippincott Company 1949), p.ix.
80   Dr. Alexis Carrel, *Man the Unknown* (Burns and Oates, London 1961), p.51.
81   Most of this information is drawn from the fine booklet, *Vivisection: Science or Sham* by Dr. Roy Kupsinel (PRISM, Anaheim California, 1990), pp.6-7.
82   Information from *GUARDIANS* Autumn 1995, p.13, who give as their source the Australian Association for Humane Research.
83   *Animal Experiments in Pharmacological Analysis* by Floyd R. Domer, Ph.D. (Charles C. Thomas, Springfield USA 1971), p.14.
84   Ibid.
85   Ibid. pp.14-15.

86   Ibid. p.15.
87   Ibid. p.16.
88   Ibid. p.19.
89   Ibid. p.21.
90   Ibid.
91   Ibid. p.23
92   Ibid. p.25.
93   Ibid. p.26.
94   Ibid. p.27.
95   Ibid. p.28.
96   Ibid. p.30.
97   Ibid.
98   Ibid. p.31.
99   Ibid. p.95.
100 Ibid. p.45.
101 Ibid. p.97.
102 Edward J. Calabrese, *Toxic Susceptibility: Male/Female Differences* (John Wiley and Sons, New York 1985), p.11.
103 Ibid.
104 Ibid. pp.12-13.
105 Domer, op. cit., p.36.
106 Ibid.
107 See Calabrese, op. cit., p.13.
108 Ibid.
109 Ibid.
110 Ibid.
111 Ibid. p.17.
112 Ibid. pp.18-19.
113 Ibid. p.20.
114 Ibid. pp.32-33.
115 Ibid. p.72.
116 Ibid. p.79.
117 Ibid. p.83.
118 Ibid. p.88.
119 Ibid. p.93.
120 Ibid. p.98.
121 Ibid. p.109.
122 Ibid. p.140.
123 Ibid. p.316.
124 Ibid. p.178.
125 Ibid. p.317.
126 Patrick Rattigan, N.D., *Cancer, Cure and Cover-Up* (Nemesis 1993),p.1.
127 Dr. John A. McDougall, M.D., in *Vegetarian Times,* Sept. 1986, quoted in Ruesch, *1,000 Doctors (and Many More) Against Vivisection* (CIVIS 1989), p.51.
128 Ruesch, ibid. p.49.
129 Dr. Vernon Coleman, *Why Animal Experiments Must Stop* (European Medical

Journal, Second Edition 1994), p.71.
130 Quoted in Coleman, op. cit., p.72.
131 Quoted by Dr. Peter Simmons in his anti-vivisection address at the Oxford Brookes Debating Society, October 6, 1993 (published by 'Doctors In Britain Against Animal Experiments' as *Debate,* 1993-1994). Source: *The Lancet,* 15 April 1972.
132 Dr. Vernon Coleman, *Betrayal of Trust* (EMJ 1994), pp.112-139.
133 Dr. Peter Simmons, op. cit. Dr. Simmons refers here to a) F J Di Carlo in *Drug Metabolism Reviews* 15: pp.409-413, 1984 and b) David Salsburg in *Fundamental and Applied Toxicology* 3: pp.63-67, 1983.
134 D.V. Parke, R.L. Smith (eds.), *Drug Metabolism From Microbe to Man* (Taylor and Francis 1977).
135 Dr. Frederick Coulston and Dr. Philippe Shubik (eds.), *Human Epidemiology and Animal Laboratory Correlations in Chemical Carcinogenesis* (Ablex, New Jersey 1980), p.1.
136 Ibid. p.17.
137 Ibid. p.9.
138 Ibid. pp.7-8.
139 Dr. Tony Chu, *You and Yours,* BBC Radio 4, 7.8.95.
140 Coulston and Shubik, op. cit., p.13.
141 Ibid. pp.13-14.
142 Ibid. p.15.
143 Ibid. p.14.
144 W E Smith et al. in *Annals of the New York Academy of Sciences* 1965, Vol.132, pp.456-488.
145 Reported on 'You and Yours', BBC radio 4, 22 December 1995.
146 Dr. H F Kraybill, 'From Mice to Men', in Coulston and Shubik, op. cit., p.31.
147 Ibid.
148 Ibid.
149 Ibid.
150 Ibid. p.39.
151 Ibid. pp.21-22.
152 Ibid. p.28.
153 Ibid. p.54.
154 Coulston and Shubik, op. cit., pp.279-280.
155 Ralph Gingell, in Coulston and Shubik, op. cit., p.95.
156 Ibid. p.105.
157 Dr. Ulrich Mohr, in Coulston and Shubik, op. cit., p.107.
158 Ibid.
159 Ibid.
160 Dr. David Clayson, in Coulston and Shubik, op. cit., p.117.
161 Dr. Shubik, op. cit., p.309.
162 Dr. Clayson, op. cit., p.390.
163 Dr. Coulston, op. cit., p.391.
164 Ibid.
165 Dr. Selikoff, Ibid.
166 Dr Clayson, ibid. p.411.

167 Dr. Upholt, ibid. p.393.
168 Dr. Coulston, ibid. p.392.
169 See Isaiah J. Fidler and Raffaella Giavazzi, 'Biologic Considerations For the Development of Animal Models to Study Treatment of Metastatic Human Neoplasms', in *Monoclonal Antibodies and Cancer Therapy* (Alan R. Liss, New York 1985), p.574.
170 Ibid. p.581.
171 Ibid. p.575.
172 Dr. Kurt Hellmann, 'Antimetastatic Drugs', in *Cancer Metastasis: Experimental and Clinical Strategies*, ed. by D.R. Welch, B.K. Bhuyan and L.A. Liotta (Alan R. Liss, New York 1986), p.3.
173 We recommend Patrick Rattigan's booklet, *Cancer, Cure and Cover-Up* (NEMESIS 1993) as an introduction to the subject. Available from UKAVIS. Also recommended is the informative *Power over Cancer* by Vernon Coleman (EMJ 1996).
174 John W. Kreider and Gerald L. Bartlett, 'Is There A Host Response to Metastasis?', in Welch et al., op. cit., p.62.
175 Interested readers should refer to the two vaccination books by Neil Z. Miller, and for more information on the damage being caused in *dogs* by vaccination the reader can contact: Catherine O'Driscoll, Canine Health Census, PO Box 1, Longnor, Derbyshire, SK17 0JD, England.
176 D.R. Welch, 'Discussion: Experimental Models of Metastasis', in Welch et al., op. cit., p.131.
177 Ibid.
178 Ibid. p.132
179 John N. Weinstein et al.: 'Regional Delivery of Monoclonal Antitumor Antibodies: Detection and Possible Treatment of Lymph Node Metastases', in Welch et al., op. cit., p.169.
180 Ibid.
181 Talmadge, ibid. p.146.
182 Ibid. p.145.
183 Nicolson, ibid. p.147.
184 J. Patrick McGovren, ibid.
185 Lance A. Liotta, ibid. p.183.
186 R.S. Kerbel, R. Liteolo, P. Frost, ibid. p.293.
187 Liotta, ibid. p.195.
188 Nicolson, ibid. p.140.
189 Vernon Coleman, *Betrayal of Trust* (EMJ 1994), p.3.
190 Dr. Hamish Cameron, *The Independent*, 26.12.95.
191 Coleman, *Betrayal of Trust*.
192 This even according to the promoters of animal 'research', the Research Defence Society, in their *RDS News* magazine for April 1995, p.17.
193 Dr. Jack Botting, ibid. p.16.
194 Ibid. p.17.
195 Hans Ruesch, *Slaughter of the Innocent*, p.361.
196 Dr. Jack Botting, *RDS News*, January 1993, p.11.
197 *The People*, 23.10.1994.

198 Junior Health Minister, Tom Sackville, advised doctors to 'restrict their use of the drug', according to the *News of the World*, 27.3.95.

199 Reported in *Daily Mirror*, 15.7.95.

200 *Take a Break*, 23.3.95.

201 'Liste von Risikomedikamenten', information sheet of Vereinigung Aerzte gegen Tierversuche, 1991.

202 See Dr. Hadwen, *The Difficulties of Dr. Deguerre*, pp.396-397.

203 Dr. Moneim A. Fadali in the Foreword to Brandon Reines' *Heart Research on Animals*, p.vi.

204 Hadwen, op. cit., pp.396 399.

205 Reines, op. cit., p.44.

206 Hadwen, op. cit., p.357.

207 *General Anaesthesia* (Fourth edition, Volume 1), ed. by T., Cecil Gray, J E Utting and John F. Nunn (Butterworths, London, Boston, etc., 1980), p.152.

208 Quoted in *A Century of Vivisection and Anti-Vivisection* by E. Westacott (Daniel 1949), p.549.

209 Ibid.

210 Ibid. p.367.

211 Quoted in Ruesch, *1,000 Doctors Against Vivisection*, pp.61-62.

212 Foreword to Reines, op. cit., p.viii.

213 Quoted in Westacott, op. cit., p.128.

214 Vernon Coleman, *Why Animal Experiments Must Stop* (EMJ 1991), pp.69-70.

215 Dr. Werner Hartinger, 'Diabetes durch Tierversuche heilbar?' (2nd edition 1991), published by Vereinigung Aerzte gegen Tierversuche, p.1.

216 Dr. H. Kief and Dr. K. Engelbar, 'Orthologie der Langerhans'schen Inseln des Menschen', in *Insulin (Teil 1)*, ed. by Eugen Doerzbach (Springer-Verlag, Berlin 1971), p.71.

217 Dr. Moses Barron, 'The Relation of the Islets of Langerhans to Diabetes with Special Reference to cases of Pancreatic Lithiasis', in *Surgery, Gynecology and Obstetrics*, Vol. XXXI, November 1920, p.444.

218 Ibid. p.447.

219 *British Medical Journal* (editorial), 4.11.22, p.882.

220 Dr. P J Cammidge, ibid. 18.11.22, p.997.

221 Dr. Ffrangcon Roberts, ibid. 16.12.22, p.1193.

222 Ibid.

223 Ibid. p.1194

224 Dr. Mark Matfield, Executive Director of the pro-vivisection Research Defence Society, on *Brian Hayes Show*, BBC Radio 2, 19.4.94.

225 *British Medical Journal*, 4 November 1922, p.833.

226 Professor John Martin, *Frontline*, Channel 4, broadcast 6.9.95.

227 Ibid.

228 Professor Martin, *Right to Reply*, Channel 4 TV programme, 16 September 1995.

229 Martin, *Frontline*.

230 Quoted in Reines, op. cit., p.30.

231 Ibid. p.27.

232 Quoted in Reines, p.9.

233 See Albert Starr and M. Lowell Edwards, 'Mitral Replacement: Clinical Experience with a Ball-Valve Prosthesis', in *Annals of Surgery* 154, 1961, p.726.
234 Ibid.
235 Ibid. p.727.
236 Ibid. p.737.
237 Ibid. p.735.
238 Ibid. p.740.
239 Ibid.
240 Ruesch, *Slaughter of the Innocent*, p.346.
241 Ibid. p.328.
242 Vernon Coleman, *How to Win Debates with Vivisectors* (EMJ 1992), p.2.
243 See Westacott, op. cit., pp.441, 625-626.
244 Richard Wagner, 'Offenes Schreiben an Herrn Ernst von Weber', *Gesammelte Schriften von Richard Wagner* (ed. by M. Balling, 1907-1923, Vol.X), p.194-195.
245 Ibid. p.199.
246 Ibid.
247 Ibid. p.200.
248 Ibid.
249 Ibid. p.208.
250 Ibid.
251 Bernard quoted in Croce, op. cit., p.103; Lister quoted in Westacott, op. cit., p.499.
252 See Marjorie Spiegel, *The Dreaded Comparison: Human and Animal Slavery* (Heretic Books, London 1988), pp.61-64.
253 Croce, op. cit., p.99.
254 'Thalidomide may inhibit proliferation mesenchyme in human limb buds', in *Analytical Cellular Pathology*, 1989. Vol, 1, p.247 quoted in 'The Truth about Embryo Research', factsheet prepared by Dr. Michael Jarmulowicz of Royal Free Hospital School of Medicine, London, August 1990.
255 *The Lancet*, 26 August 1995, p.566.
256 Coleman, *How to Win Debates with Vivisectors*, p.12.
257 The words of Orrin Hatch, from *Big Science*, BBC2 TV, 18.7.95.
258 Ibid.
259 Ibid.
260 Ibid.
261 *The Lancet*, 23.9.5, p.847.
262 *Whose Mind Is It Anyway?* BBC2 TV, 25.4.95.
263 Ibid.
264 Ibid.
265 Ibid.
266 Coulston, op. cit. p.373.
267 *Anti-Slavery International Annual Report 1994-1995*, p.10.
268 Official letter from Dr. Mark Matfield, dated 14 July 1995, to C. Zdesar.
269 Official letter from Dr. Mark Matfield, dated 6 January 1995, to C. Zdesar.
270 The court records for 2 February 1970, quoted by Dr. Werner Hartinger in

CIVIS International Foundation Report, Number 11, p.3.
271 Dr. Mark Matfield on the *Brian Hayes Show*, BBC Radio 2, 19.4.94.
272 London Talkback Radio, 25.8.95.
273 Dr. Mark Matfield on the *Brian Hayes Show*, BBC Radio 2, 19.4.94.
274 *RDS News*, July 1995, p.7.
275 C.P. Page and E.M. Minshall, 'Towards chronic animal models of asthma', in *European Respiratory Review* 1995, 5:29, p.238.
276 *Heart of the Matter*, BBC Television, 6 July 1995.
277 Page and Minshall, op. cit., p.241.
278 K.F. Chung, 'Usefulness of animal models in asthma research' in *Eur.Respir.Rev.* 1995, 5: 29, p.184.
279 *Annual Report of RDS*, November 1995, p.14.
280 Zbinden, 'Applied Therapeutics', 1966, 8, pp.128-133.
281 Said at a scientific workshop held at the Ciba Foundation in London, 1989. Also stated in: *Animal Toxicity Studies: Their Relevance to Man,* ed. Lumley and Walker (Quay 1989), pp.57-67. I am indebted to the veterinary surgeon, Dr. André Menache, for this gem.
282 *Developmental Toxicology: Mechanisms and Risk*, ed. by John A. McLachlan, Robert M. Pratt and Clement L. Markert (Cold Spring Harbour 1987), p.313.
283 Ibid.
284 Ibid. p.320
285 Samuel V. Molinary, 'Preclinical Studies of Aspartame in Nonprimate Animals', in *Aspartame: Physiology and Biochemistry*, ed. by Lewis D. Stegnik and L.J. Filer (Marcel Denker Inc. 1984), pp.294-295.
286 Quoted in *Prevailing Winds* (Issue 1), 1994, p.47.
287 *Sunday Times*, 17.9.95.
288 *The Moral Maze*, BBC Radio 4, 7.12.95.
289 Steve Beddard, *Transplants* (Arc Print, London 1989), p.11.
290 Quoted in Hans Ruesch, *Naked Empress* (CIVIS 1982), p.149.
291 Ibid.
292 Professor Nick Hasstie, *MPs in Genes*, BBC2 TV, January 1995.
293 *First Sight: A Fine Line*, BBC2 TV, 9.11.95.
294 Ibid.
295 *The Lancet*, 16.9.95, p.766.
296 Ibid.
297 *The Guardian*, 19.12.95.
298 *News at Ten*, ITV, 18.12.95.
299 *The Lancet*, 26.8.95, p.570.
300 'Genetic Engineering: Hope or Hoax?', in *Third World Resurgence*, January 1995, pp.28-29.
301 Ibid.
302 Ibid.
303 *The Vivisection Problem of Today (1926)*, p.8.
304 Ibid.

The Power in Our Hands
Neighbourhood based, world shaking
Tony Gibson

Tony Gibson matches the capacities of ordinary people doing extraordinary things with our prospects for survival. Drawing on countless historical and present-day examples of individuals and groups doing their own thing, pooling resources, re-writing the rules and saying Enough is enough! — from the Grameen Bank in Bangladesh to the Rochdale Pioneers, from Ken Saro-Wiwa to Tom Paine and Emma Must — he shows how the potential for change and success lies in basic human assets: the creative instinct to do things ourselves; the staying power that comes from working together on the same footing and sharing the credit; the inborn urge to ask why? and then how?; the support we get from family and community; and that great human asset, time on our hands.

He shows how too much talk gets in the way of practical action, and outlines ways to bring about changes, from the ground up; developing working relation-ships through which we can regain control of our lives, linking up with others, near and far, who bring the same basic human resources to bear on the problem / opportunity they face.

The book concludes with a discussion of working models for change at neigh-bourhood level and the working relationships they engender, drawing on the resourcefulness and willingness of ordinary people to improve their own lives and the condition of their neighbourhood.

"This book is invaluable... a joy. I find it inspiring... He hits his target and does so in a manner the reader can never forget."   From the Foreword by Lord Scarman
"This is the missing link in the debate about how we live, the secret formula that our leaders consistently misunderstand, Tony Gibson's book is about people and power and how the grassroots can effect real change. It's vital!" John Vidal, *The Guardian*

£10 pbk 320pp illustrated 1 897766 28 9

If you cannot find these books in your local bookshop, you may order them post free from the publisher. Please send your payment to
Jon Carpenter Publishing, The Spendlove Centre, Charlbury OX7 3PQ
(phone/fax 01608 811969).

Ethical Investment
A saver's guide
Peter Lang

The book for anyone with money to invest — whether a few hundred pounds, or many thousands — who tries to apply ethical standards to their everyday life, but who doesn't have a detailed understanding of money and investment. Written in everyday language, free of the jargon of the financial world.

Unlike the typical financial adviser, the author explains and describes all the ethical investment opportunities, including those that don't pay a commission to 'independent financial advisers' for recommending them. These include banks, building societies, and a number of funds and companies in the so-called 'social economy', as well as the commission-paying unit trusts, PEPs and pension funds. There is also a discussion of the choice of insurance companies.

Ethical Investment explains how all these various investments operate, their ethical pros and cons, and guides the investor through the questions that need to be asked before deciding whether to sign on the dotted line.

Peter Lang pulls no punches in revealing

• why 'independent' financial advisers are not independent in the way you might think

• why financial advisers are extremely selective in the investments they recommend

• why many investment opportunities sold as 'ethical' are far from ethical

• why pensions are unlikely to keep you in old age in the manner the brochures suggest

• why a pension may not give you the best income in retirement

• why the best investment for your future might be to spend rather than save

• how companies make massive deductions from the money you invest

• the widely differing ethical criteria used by different 'ethical' funds

• where to find the information you need to judge a company's ethical record

Peter Lang is an environmental consultant and writer. He is the author of *Lets Work: Rebuilding the local economy*, the definitive guide to setting up and running LETS (Local Exchange Trading Systems). He is currently helping set up Britain's first ethical property company.

£10 pbk   192pp   1 897766 20 3

Low Impact Development
Planning and people in a sustainable countryside
Simon Fairlie

This complete re-examination of Britain's planning system from the bottom up – from the point of view of the planned, rather than of the planner – is an important contribution to the topical debate about the future and use of' the countryside and what it means to achieve sustainability in the modern world.

Simon Fairlie argues that instead of excluding low income people from living and working in rural areas, planners should look favourably on proposals for low impact, environmentally benign homes and workplaces in the open countryside. Criteria for planning approval at present favour the wealthy commuter and the large-scale farmer and discriminate heavily against (e.g.) smallholders, low-impact homes, and experimental forms of husbandry.

The book is the result of much detailed research. It includes a number of cases studies of low impact developments, some of which received permission, some of which failed. It includes illustrations; policy recommendations; guides to acts of parliament, government circulars and policy guidelines etc.; references; and explanatory appendices. It is an invaluable tool both for those who wish to live on the land in a sustainable manner, and for planners and politicians who would like to make it possible for them to do so. As well as proposing changes to planning law, the author shows how existing regulations can be used to enable many environmentally benign projects to take place.

Simon Fairlie is an editor of *The Ecologist*, and co-author of *Whose Common Future?* (Earthscan, 1993). He writes for *The Guardian, New Statesman and Society*, and *Perspectives*.

£10 paperback 1 897766 25 4 176pp illustrated

If you cannot find these books in your local bookshop, you may order
them post free from the publisher. Please send your payment to
Jon Carpenter Publishing, The Spendlove Centre, Charlbury OX7 3PQ
(phone/fax 01608 811969).

Homelessness: What Can Be Done
An immediate programme of self-help and mutual aid
Ron Bailey

A practical programme for the provision of homes for the homeless, from one of the country's most experienced campaigners for the underprivileged.

Despite current financial constraints, the author shows how money, land and labour are available now to start a massive programme of housing provision for all homeless people. His proposals would get homeless families out of bed and breakfast, rescue single homeless people from their cardboard cities, and provide decent emergency housing for hundreds of thousands of forgotten people.

Ron Bailey argues that central and local government cannot solve the problem of homelessness. Instead, he claims, the energy and enthusiasm of the homeless themselves can be harnessed in a massive self-build programme. The role of local government is to facilitate this effort.

The book is also intensely practical. It shows exactly how these homes can be built, where such large sums of money will come from, and where the land is.

By studying vacant land registers held by over 120 local authorities, by showing exactly where—from existing council budgets—the cash could come from, and by explaining how the homeless can be motivated and organised, Bailey comes up with a costed strategy for dealing with homelessness in urban inner-city areas, small towns and rural areas alike.

The book rejects the government's approach of 'mutual hostility' and proposes instead a programme of mutual aid between government at all levels and the homeless. It includes some simple policy changes whereby central government could facilitate the process.

Ron Bailey started the present squatting movement in 1968 as part of a successful campaign to persuade local authorities to hand over empty houses to self-help groups of homeless people. He documented these events in a Penguin Special, *The Squatters*. In the 1970s he launched Shelter's campaign to get responsibility for homeless families shifted to housing departments (*The Grief Report*, 1972): another success story. And in 1975 (*The Homeless and the Empty Houses*, Penguin Special) he devised a whole new method of funding the renovation of empty houses—which is also now accepted policy.

£7.99 paperback 112pp ISBN 1 897766 09 2

Reinventing the Economy

The Third Way
David Simmons

How Margaret Thatcher and, after her, John Major have traded on popular disillusionment with socialism and a deliberate falsification of what Keynes was saying to discredit the left-of-centre consensus in Britain today and impose an unjust economic and social system that has but one objective: to re-allocate wealth from the lower and middle income groups to the already wealthy, by making ninety per cent of people worse off. This has been done at the expense of the job security and welfare of the overwhelming majority.

The New Right cannot succeed in its claimed goal of creating wealth for all in a competitive market economy, as it is neither interested in, nor relevant to, the concerns of economic and social justice. Yet many people have come to believe that because socialism has been discredited, the political philosophy of the New Right is the only possible option.

Simmons' original contribution to contemporary economic debate is to show that this is not true.

While other writers have set out to demonstrate the failure of the New Right, Simmons goes further: he shows that since the Keynesian consensus did not fail, but was merely replaced by politicians with different priorities, there is an alternative. This can be found in the nature of government itself in a liberal democracy, in the consensus that already exists among voters, and in the example of those countries where different strategies are in place and working successfully. Liberal democracy, by definition, is concerned with the welfare of all. And among the population at large, there is a clear consensus in favour of established left-of-centre policies: the welfare state, government intervention in the economy, Keynesian demand management and so on. The consensus is within the range of traditional Labour policies, and any party offering an alternative to the New Right should take this on board.

The evidence shows that this programme is proven to be effective in creating a socially and economically healthy society.

"A powerful indictment of New Right policies."   Professor Masato Oka, Yokohama City University

David Simmons is a former Lecturer in Economics and the author of several books. Economic Power was praised by Leopold Kohr for its 'careful scholarship, the soundness of its economics'.

£11.99 paperback 1 897766 17 3   288 pages

VDU Terminal Sickness

Computer Health Risks and How to Protect Yourself

Peggy Bentham

A new edition of this pioneering analysis of the health problems faced by computer users.

The subjects addressed include the design hazards of computers themselves, the health implications of working environments (including chair design, noise, lighting and sick building syndrome), and the numerous different sicknesses and muscoloskeletal injuries reported among users.

A new Part 5 covers new mandatory safety standards; recent studies of cancer risks; and changes in employment law, insurance, and so on. Latest European requirements are fully covered.

This book is essential jargon-free reading for employers and employees, as well as for people who use a computer at home and parents whose children play computer games. The safety information is also essential for schools.

- 'It's recommended reading, especially for people who already have health symptoms or suspect they may have a dodgy VDU.' Jack Schofield, *The Guardian*
- 'Brilliant text and research.' Anne Arnold Silk, consultant optician
- 'An essential handbook for all of us concerned with the magic screen.' *Glasgow Herald*
- 'Recommended reading for all concerned with VDU health risks.' Liz Hodgkinson, *The Guardian*
- 'Most importantly, this book offers practical advice to employers and employees on how to meet the new EC standards, avoid the health risks and use VDUs and computers *safely.*' *BIFU Report*, Banking, Insurance and Finance Union

Peggy Bentham is a research scientist, consultant and writer. She has represented the British Institute of Management on a government information technology project.

£12.99 240pp pbk ISBN 1 897766 21 1

If you cannot find these books in your local bookshop, you may order them post free from the publisher. Please send your payment to Jon Carpenter Publishing, The Spendlove Centre, Charlbury OX7 3PQ (phone/fax 01608 811969).

Animal Rights

Extending the circle of compassion
Mark Gold

Essential reading for all those concerned about the treatment of animals. It discusses the extremely topical issues of cruel farming practices, live animal transportation, and the increasing trend towards meat-free diets.

• the most up-to-date and authoritative exposition of animal rights and the vegetarian and vegan case.

• provocatively links cruelty towards animals with a failure by humans to respect their own kind, demolishing the myth that animal rights campaigners care more about animals than about humans. Mark Gold shows how concern for animal welfare and animal rights has sprung from concern for human welfare and human rights, and gives examples to show how champions of the one have always been champions of the other too.

• an indictment of the violent and neo-fascist minorities who have tried to hijack the cause

• a telling analysis of the achievements of the last twenty years and a thought-provoking insight into both the problems and possibilities for future progress.

• persuasive evidence, advice and encouragement to help readers to make their own contribution towards a world where animals are treated with the respect they deserve. Extensive resource listings.

As Director of Animal Aid for the last decade and a campaign organiser for Compassion In World Farming before that, Mark Gold is uniquely qualified to present the truth behind what has become one of the most fiercely debated issues of our age. He is also author of the very successful *Living Without Cruelty.*

£7.99 pbk   160pp   1 897766 16 5

Towards a Sustainable Economy

The need for fundamental change
Ted Trainer

A lucid and hard-hitting analysis of the truth about our economic system that explains precisely why a few people are getting richer, most people are getting poorer, and why – if we don't change our ways – we're all heading for global catastrophe. Mass poverty and hunger, unemployment, under-development, waste, armed conflict, resource scarcity and environmental destruction — all are caused by the disastrous flaws in our economy.

Ted Trainer shows how economic growth is seriously mistaken because it ignores finite resource and ecological limits, thereby promoting violence and injustice as well as ecological calamity.

Having invalidated both 'free enterprise capitalism' and 'big state socialism' as viable long-term economic systems, Dr Trainer puts forward an alternative, a Third Way 'conserver society' that includes some of the best elements of the other two. His argument is that an economy for a sustainable world order must involve simpler living standards, a high degree of local economic self-sufficiency and therefore much less transport and travel, a much smaller cash sector of the economy, more cooperative arrangements such as town banks and working bees, and many free goods from Permaculture-designed 'edible landscapes'.

The 'limits to growth' are as real as ever, and we ignore them at our peril.

Ted Trainer's previous books include *Abandon Affluence!* ("Spares no illusions" – *The Ecologist*) and *The Conserver Society* (both Zed Books) and *Developed to Death* (Green Print, now in its third printing).

£10.99 192pp paperback 1 897766 14 9

If you cannot find these books in your local bookshop, you may order them post free from the publisher. Please send your payment to Jon Carpenter Publishing, The Spendlove Centre, Charlbury OX7 3PQ (phone/fax 01608 811969).

FREE CATALOGUES

Catalogues of books published and distributed by
Jon Carpenter are available from:

**Jon Carpenter Publishing, The Spendlove Centre,
Charlbury, OX7 3PQ**

We also have a specialist catalogue of books and booklets on
vegetarian and vegan food and travel, organic gardening,
animal rights, alternative technology, health and green living.

We look forward to hearing from you.